5 Acres & A Dream The Book

5 Acres & A Dream The Book

The Challenges of Establishing a Self-Sufficient Homestead

Leigh Tate

Kikobian Books
www.Kikobian.com

While this book is mostly the telling of our homesteading experiences, I have tried to include useful information for interested readers. I have made every effort to make sure that this information is accurate and up-to-date at the time of publication. If you do find errors, please be kind. They are not intentional and I am still researching and learning. In fact, some things may be out-of-date by the time you read this book. That being said, please do, thoroughly research information that is new to you before utilizing it. Please make certain it is correct, appropriate, and applicable to your situation.

This book was built, from the ground up, with open source software on an open source operating system: Ubuntu Linux 12.04 (Precise Pangolin), Xfce 4.8 and 4.10 Desktop Environments, LibreOffice 3.5.7.2 (Writer word processor and Calc spreadsheet), Notes 1.7.7 quick notes plugin, Leafpad 0.8.18.1 text editor, Gimp 2.8 photo editor, Inkscape 0.48 vector drawing program, Agave 0.4.7 colorscheme designer, and Scribus desktop publisher versions 1.4 and 1.5. Also used were open source fonts Lobster 1.4, EB Garamond, EB Garamond SC (SIL Open Font License Version 1.1.), and Liberation Sans (GNU General Public License v.2).

ISBN 978-0-9897111-0-4

Kikobian Books
www.kikobian.com

This book is dedicated to the readers of my blog
5acresandadream.com.
Without you all, it never would have happened.

Contents

ACKNOWLEDGMENTS

Behind every big project there are people who never make the spotlight. Yet, without them, the project wouldn't have made it. This book has been a huge project for me, and there are several people who made it possible. I owe them my most sincere thanks.

I would like to thank Benita Story (www.basicallybenita.com), who was the first to suggest that I turn my blog into a book. I didn't take it seriously at first, but thanks to her gentle prodding, this book has finally come into being. I want to thank her for her continued encouragements, for generously offering her editorial skills, for her suggestions and technical help, and for introducing me to the world of self-publishing.

Thank you to my husband, Dan, who was enthusiastic about the project from the beginning. I want to thank him for his prayers and ever-encouraging support. He was always willing to read, brainstorm, and discuss each chapter with me. I also want to thank him for his suggestions and help with the photographs.

Thank you to my son and daughter-in-law, Nolan and Leigh Anne East. They proof-read, offered suggestions, asked the right questions, and helped me clarify what I was trying to say.

Thank you to Karen of Fairview Farm, who is the "internet acquaintance" mentioned in Chapter 7. In truth, she has been more than that. She has been a mentor to me as I set out to learn what it would take to feed our animals from our land. She has offered information and pointed me toward resources that have been invaluable.

Finally, thank you to my blog readers. It was your interest that shaped this book. Your comments, questions, visits to particular posts, even the search terms you used to find me, all contributed to the content of this book. It seemed that every time I became discouraged with the writing of it, one of you would email me and suggest I write a book! Thank you for your encouragement. Thank you for making me a part of your internet lives.

INTRODUCTION

This is not a "how-to" book. Neither is it a "why to" book. This book is about two people having a dream and taking the first step toward it, then another, and another. It's about a journey. It's about learning what it takes to make a go at homesteading. Like most long-distance journeys, it requires a destination and preparation. It starts slowly and picks up momentum along the way. It often makes wrong turns, runs into dead ends, takes detours and at this point, we have not arrived. We are in route.

Many people start the homesteading journey, or at least want to start the journey, and for many reasons. It was one of the things I noticed when I started reading homesteading blogs. In preparation for this book, I queried my own blog readers, asking them why they homesteaded or were interested in homesteading. Here is a list of most of those reasons. They are not in any particular order.

> concern about the food supply
> to know where their food comes from and what's in it
> to be able to eat nutritious, quality, real food
> to save the environment
> to save the earth
> to combat climate change
> to reduce their carbon footprint
> peak oil
> every little bit helps
> to not be dependent on the government
> to not be dependent on the consumer system
> to become self-sufficient
> to feel productive
> for a simpler life
> more economical living
> healthier living
> sustainable living
> quieter life
> less wasteful life
> to get out of the rat race
> to live in the country
> desire for more solitude

religious separation from materialism
love the lifestyle
to preserve historical skills and heritage animal breeds
to set an example to others
to develop a true sense of interdependent community
preparedness
collapse of western civilization as we know it
collapse of industrialism
collapse of our monetary system
collapse of our economic system
collapse of the United States
love of the natural world
to establish a connection with the earth
personal identity: "I was born to do this," "it's in my blood"

Probably one or another item on that list will strike a chord with you, while others will seem downright silly. There are probably other reasons but for most homesteaders, there will be multiple reasons as to why they choose to homestead. Since this book is not about why you should homestead, I'm not going to discuss or debate any of these. I mention them, however, because they do play an important role in our homesteading journey.

It is on an individual level that our reasons are important, because what they provide is motivation. Motivation is key to getting started and key to staying the course. It dominates our beginnings and resurges with our successes. It dissolves into discouragement when things go wrong. Because of that, motivation by itself isn't enough. It gives us the enthusiasm to get started, and will often help us along the way, but there's more to it than that. We also need commitment.

Commitment is what keeps us going when we don't feel like it. Commitment is a choice of will, not an emotion. It is vital to our homesteading success when problems arise or things go wrong. In a way, one could say it's the true test of our resolve to do what we set out to do.

At this point, my husband Dan and I are about four and a half years into establishing our homestead. It's not long enough to tell you that if we succeed, you can succeed too. It's recent enough, however, that the challenges of getting started are still fresh in our minds. Since it's a personal account, some of it might be helpful and of interest to you, some of it may not. I'll leave that for you to decide.

Chapter 1

The Dream

"5 Acres & A Dream." There is no specific point that either my husband Dan or I can pinpoint as being the birth and definition of our dream. In vague terms, our dream has always been to have our own land and the ability to meet our needs from it. It wasn't motivated by any environmental or political concern; in fact, we were thinking about this long before anyone thought carbon was a problem or being "green" was the right thing to do.

Rather, it has been an attraction to a way of life, to what we thought would be more fulfilling and personally more productive than the typical lifestyle of our culture.

For Dan, I think it started as a child. His father was a hard worker and a good provider. While not wealthy by American standards, everyone in the family had their own TV, their own car, a family swimming pool, and steak for dinner once a week. Money and material goods flowed through his father's hands like water. Growing up, Dan observed all this and participated in the fruits of his father's labors. But one thing he observed, which influenced him profoundly, was the realization that in spite of his money and what he owned, none of it made his father truly happy.

For myself, some of my favorite childhood memories are of family hikes and camping trips. Our lifestyle was a frugal one which frustrated my mother, but my father seemed content. When the back-to-the-land movement hit in the 1970s, I dropped out of college and jumped on board. With a small group of friends, we bought 140 undeveloped, forested, mountain acres in the Ozarks. We had no road access, no electricity, and no clocks. We were determined to do everything by hand, and so we began. Eventually, interpersonal conflicts took their toll. I was one of the ones who left, but the desire for the lifestyle never left me.

When Dan and I got together in the early 1990s, we had a number of things in common. We were spiritually compatible, had similar interests, and both felt a pull toward a lifestyle different than the one we were living. Neither of us was interested in making a fortune, following the latest trends, nor in acquiring hoards of material goods. A life of entertainment and ease did not appeal to us. Rather, we both liked working with our hands and being outdoors. We both longed for a simpler life, a life that gave us a sense of purpose, appreciation, and satisfaction with what we do and how we do it. We wanted a place of our own, a niche we could cut out from the rest of the world, a lifestyle that relied less on consumerism and more on our relationship with the natural creation and its gifts. In short, we wanted out of the rat race.

This did not produce any major lifestyle changes immediately. In the beginning, it was more of a vague idea and feeling of what we wanted. We knew the general direction in which we wanted to head, but realized there were obstacles as well.

The biggest obstacle was money. Since neither of us was interested in accumulating wealth, there was no large savings stashed away with which to get started. There was no large expensive home to sell for capital gains to reinvest. We could have both worked our tails off to accumulate enough to buy what we wanted, but our priorities dictated that we make other choices. The most important choice was to homeschool our children. This meant being a one-income family, and on an income most folks wouldn't consider sufficient for one person, let alone four. It was both a personal conviction, as well as a sense of spiritual accountability, that enabled us to make the financial sacrifice. Now that our children are adults and on their own, I can honestly say that we have no regrets.

Still, these choices meant living paycheck to paycheck, on rental property, and always with a longing for a place of our own. That's not to say that we didn't look for such a place from time to time all those years. We would look at land, at houses, and at price tags. Dan was loathe to get a mortgage, since we are both committed to being debt free, but there didn't seem to be any way around that. Then, too, there was a down payment, although that was before the 2008 mortgage crisis when workarounds were common. Still, we couldn't afford a mortgage payment higher than our $450 monthly rent, so we stayed put.

Not having our own land didn't stop us from pursuing certain aspects of a homesteading lifestyle, however. We had a large vegetable garden, preserved all of our vegetables, most of our fruit and some of our meat. We bought much of our food in bulk through a buying cooperative, kept a large food and water storage, heated with wood, and lived without air conditioning, cell phones, and cable TV. Homesteading lends itself quite well to homeschooling, and much of our curricula was built around 4-H project books covering nature, gardening, cooking, woodworking, and other hands-on skills. Everybody in the family chipped in.

Besides work, we had leisure time as well. Although this was before television went digital, our reception was limited in the mountains, so we did not rely on it for entertainment. Instead, in the evenings, we would read. Dan would read aloud while the rest of us listened and did quiet hand projects. We especially enjoyed Laura Ingalls Wilders' *Little House on the Prairie* series, and Ralph Moody's *Little Britches* books. Also Eric Sloane's books, especially *Diary of An Early American Boy*. The simple lifestyles and down-to-earth practicality portrayed in these books did much to keep our dream alive. We saw that it was indeed possible to be content with a less materialistic way of living.

Personal reading did much to foster our dream as well. While Dan read *Five Acres and Independence* by Maurice G. Kains, I read Carla Emery's *Encyclopedia of Country Living.* Both of these books brought a practical, more modern application to what we read in the *Little House* and *Little Britches* books. In addition, we began to collect Eric Sloane's books, such as *A Reverence for Wood* and *The Seasons of America Past.* We found a wealth of agrarian wisdom and common sense ideas we could put into practice. The more we read, the more doable our dream seemed.

Eventually, the children grew up and worked their way through college. A family illness resulted in two long distance moves for Dan and me, but eventually we returned to the foothills of the Blue Ridge Mountains. We ended up in a small apartment in a small city, with no money and nowhere else to go.

Urban apartment dwelling confirmed two things: One, we didn't like the typical modern lifestyle, and two, we wanted out. Money was still a problem during this time, but we did start to plan and began to weigh our options. Not having a mortgage seemed out of the question. Still, we were either going to have a mortgage payment or pay rent. We had less control over rent, plus the place wasn't ours to do what we wanted.

The first question was what price range would be affordable for us? We started with a figure we felt would be a comfortable monthly mortgage payment and worked backwards from there, to find a price range. We considered two options: to either buy land and build, or buy a place that needed some work but had the land we wanted.

Finding land to buy wasn't as easy as we'd hoped. Even though we were in a relatively rural area, the southern Appalachians in recent years, had become the target destination of well-off retirees. Many of these were northerners who originally moved to Florida, but for one reason or another didn't like it there. Rather than return to the north, they moved to the middle latitudes of the Eastern U.S. Dan referred to these folks as "halfbacks" because they moved halfway back north. In the mountains especially, they had beautiful surroundings, lots of touristy things to do, a change of seasons but with mild winters and summers, and more economical living than from where they had come. The problem with this was that land prices skyrocketed. Larger acreage was parceled out into large 1 to 10 acre expensive lots associated with a development, and with building restrictions to go along with that fancy price tag.

Our other option was to buy several acres with an old house or mobile home already on it. Dan was less keen on this one, as he'd always had a hankering to build a log home. Actually, I did too, but between the price of land and the price of log home kits, I figured nothing short of a miracle would enable us to go that route. I just wanted to keep my options open.

We had two ways to go here, too: buy a newer home, which would need fewer repairs but have a higher mortgage payment, or buy a fixer-upper, have lower payments, and work on it as we were financially able. Unfortunately, most homes in our price range with a few acres were such serious fixer-uppers as to not be inhabitable, or else they were not in good locations. They were either in very public, high traffic areas, or surrounded by acres of man-made eyesores and other forms of havoc wreaked upon the land.

Since we had a better chance of winning the lottery than approaching a six digit income, our financial outlook in regards to what we could buy remained bleak. Yes, we were finally able to save, but even that was slow going and, as Dan used to say, we weren't getting any younger. To keep from getting too discouraged, we would sit down, from time to time to discuss and fine tune our dream.

Because of finances, the thing we had to redefine was the minimum acreage we wanted. If we were being realistic, 100, 60, 40, even 10 acres was out. We could have looked elsewhere, in another state, but without the cash to buy outright, getting a mortgage required having a job in whatever area we chose to live. And with loans getting harder to obtain, that meant having a stable job, not a new job. Relocating and starting over was an option, but the last one on the list.

A piece of land as private and remote as possible was also out. It just didn't seem to exist where we were, except in exotic, expensive retirement developments. And if we couldn't afford the acreage to surround ourselves with peace and quiet, then we would have to accept the idea of having neighbors.

During this time, I would check the online real estate listings every day. If anything of interest popped up during the week, we would do a drive-by as soon as we could. Things that looked good in real estate photos, turned out not so good in person. Some were located on noisy, busy roads; some

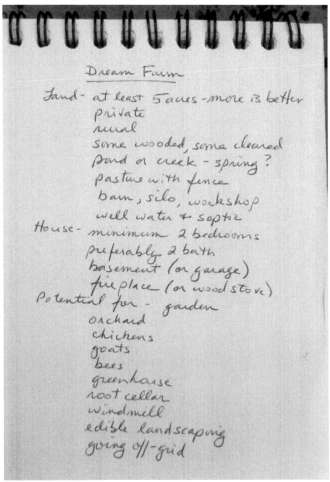

We spent many evenings discussing our dream farm

were surrounded by unkempt homes with piles of trash in the yard; some had houses with serious structural damage; sometimes the land was too steep; a few had huge electric towers cutting across the property; sometimes the drive would have been too long for Dan to get to work. If we did find something we were interested in, it always seemed to have just come under contract, as though everyone else was looking for the exact same thing we were.

One thing we learned was that in our state at least, mobile homes, though much less expensive, were not treated the same as "stick built" homes by the mortgage industry. Conventional homes were considered investments, while mobile homes depreciated like vehicles. We learned this when we tried to buy one. It was the land rather than the home we were interested in, five beautiful, private acres bordering a year round creek. We figured we could live in the mobile home until we could build our dream home. We were told we could only get a 10-year term, because the home was nearly 20 years old. Lenders considered that once it was 30 years of age, its value would have depreciated to $0. As a mobile home, they would only give us a loan for as long as it had value.

Interest rates on mobile homes were much higher as well. This actually offset the lower selling price, so that the monthly payments would have been the same as for a stick-built house.

Then, too, mobile homes could not be sold unless they passed inspection by the county building inspector. This was really the death of one deal, because the owners had done repairs that didn't meet code. They claimed they couldn't afford to fix them and hinted that we could have the repairs done. However, we knew better than to sink a lot of money into a home to which we didn't hold the deed.

Behind that particular property was an adjacent five, undeveloped acres. It bordered the same creek and was cheap ($3200 an acre). It was also available, and we liked the idea of a 10-acre homestead. Trying to purchase this property, however, became another problem. Land in this part of the country is sold with the developer's mindset. This means there is a much higher interest rate and much shorter terms (usually only several years), because it is expected that the buyer will quickly take out a home building loan and use part of it to pay off the land. The idea that we wanted to put the two pieces of property together, didn't make sense to the loan officer at the bank. She had a good reputation, but was apparently only familiar with building lots, not country property. To us, the idea was simple: 5 acres + 5 acres = a 10 acre homestead. She didn't get it.

To help explain what we wanted to do, we showed her the plat map for the two properties, which we obtained from the county registrar of deeds. A plat map shows the legal boundaries of a property, as well as roads and easements. The bank officer only saw that there was no road access to the undeveloped five acres and became alarmed. In fact, she was convinced it was illegal to sell land without a road to it. Even though both the plat map and the deed stipulated a 15 foot right-of-way on either side of the property line, she sent letters to the surrounding land owners demanding a 30 foot right-of-way on either side. That was asking for a total easement of 60 feet, twice what was already allowed. No one would sign! We wouldn't have either if we'd been one of them, since the right-of-way was already granted. For us, it was unsettling to think we were getting off on the wrong foot with neighbors we had not yet met.

We tried repeatedly to clarify our goals and motives. Her response to our explanations was always "What if...?"; mostly, what if we wanted to sell it. She never did understand that we wanted it because we didn't want anyone else to buy it! It was both a privacy issue and a land usage issue. We had plans for that land. What we didn't realize at the time is that hers was the modern mindset about property: it isn't for living on, it's for investing in. In the end, that deal fell through as well.

During our time of looking, the 2008 mortgage crisis hit. Like other potential buyers, we felt this worked in our favor because housing prices dropped and so did interest rates. What we expected was for land prices to drop as well, but they never did. As housing prices spiraled downward, land prices remained the same - high.

As time passed, our dream list began to change. We'd been looking for nearly three years, but nothing came close to our dream property. We began to entertain smaller pieces of land, down to an acre, and in more urban areas. We were less fussy about how many rooms the house had, if it had a fireplace, or whether or not the property had outbuildings. Finally, in March 2009, the place we eventually bought came on the market.

1920's farmhouse on 5 acres. Hardwood floors. Ceramic tile on kitchen floor. Bedrooms & kitchen have the original plank walls. Claw foot tub, screened front porch, quaint outbuildings, large trees, and beautiful setting. Needs work but so much potential in this unpolished jewel!!!!!!!!

We did a drive-by the next day. It was just outside town limits but not as private as I had hoped. Still, the surrounding homes were traditional brick with well-kept yards. The road, ironically, was quiet. I say ironically, because if its usual work and school traffic had been present when we first looked at it, I would have nixed it as too busy.

Within two days we had made an offer. The following day we learned someone else had made an offer as well. I'm sure the sellers were hoping for a bidding war, but Dan had his mind set firmly on our limit, and would only counteroffer for that amount. The other buyers won the contract.

This was very disappointing because the property had much of the potential we wanted. It had the acreage, both cleared and wooded. The house seemed absolutely perfect for us. It had two bathrooms, two bedrooms, and a sunroom which could double as a bedroom because it had a closet (if it has a closet, it's a bedroom in real estate terms). It had a pantry, an office space added on to the back, a screened-in front porch, a closed-in back porch/laundry room, and two fireplaces. It didn't have a basement but it had a carport and two old outbuildings. It wasn't in an eyesore neighborhood and the road was not a throughway except for local homeowners. It definitely needed work, but not so much that we couldn't move in immediately. We had looked at a lot of homes that had deteriorated to uninhabitable, and this one was definitely better than that.

About three of the five acres were cleared, the rest were wooded.

Above: The living room. It had the fireplace we had wanted and I loved all the French doors. The single French door opens into the hallway. The double doors on the right open into the dining room. A hardwood floor was hidden under a hideous, wall-to-wall pink carpet. The walls and ceiling are painted cement board.

Left: Front Bedroom. The fireplace is back to back with the fireplace in the living room. Both use the same chimney and were fitted with grates for burning coal. The walls, ceilings, and floors in the two bedrooms are tongue and groove.

Above: The sun room, with nine large single paned windows, all original to the house. Located off the living room through double French doors, it was perfect for my weaving and fiber studio. The "pie pan" on the wall in the corner is actually a flue cover and hides an old stove pipe hole. The home was originally heated with coal and there is evidence of stove locations in every room of the house.

Right: The hall bathroom with original clawfoot tub, sink, and medicine cabinet. The vinyl flooring was a fairly recent addition, but the window was original, as were the tongue & groove walls and ceiling.

Right: At 180 square feet, the kitchen was small and unappealing. It had been remodeled previously, but remained outdated. The tongue and groove ceiling and walls were original, but the windows had been replaced as had the floor. Its ceramic tiles were now uneven, cracked, broken, and grimy. Countertop and cabinet space were woefully inadequate. An old, rusted out dishwasher didn't work. The one wall cabinet (above fridge on the right) was too high to reach. Also note the circuit breaker box, then located behind the refrigerator.

Left, the other side of the kitchen. The post featured in the photo was added after a load bearing wall had been removed to enlarge the original 11.5 foot by 11.5 foot kitchen. Being somewhat in the middle of the room, it was very much in the way. Nothing in the room was a standard size including the handmade wall cabinets and the 29 inch by 76 inch back door. The wall under the window showed rain damage and the casing of the window itself was broken. As much potential as the rest of the house had, the kitchen was the most challenging to visualize as anything other than a disaster.

Above: The dining room. The French doors open to the living room and like the living room, the walls are painted cement board. Shown above is one of two corner cabinets, both built-in. In the hallway, note the telephone cubby. The dining room, living room, and hallway all had wall-to-wall pink carpeting.

Right: The back porch sported jalousie windows. It struck me as odd that the back door opened out, instead of into the room as is customary for exterior doors. Previously used as a laundry and mud room, I could envision the porch as my summer and canning kitchen too.

The property had two outbuildings, built about the same time as the house.

A couple of weeks went by as we steeled ourselves for another round of looking. The emotional cost of trying to buy a home does take its toll and we needed to regroup. About the time we were ready to start again, our realtor called and excitedly told us that the first contract had fallen through. Were we still interested? They had accepted our offering price, partly on the strength that we had been pre-approved for the amount we offered. All we had to do was formalize the contract.

The initial reason given for the failure of the first contract was problems with financing. Later, we found out that after they had the home inspected, they felt too many repairs were needed and had backed out of the contract. We did get a copy of the inspection they had done, and yes, the house needed some immediate major repairs. Between our savings and a small inheritance I had received recently, we felt that we could afford a 30% down payment and still have enough for the most urgent repairs. We signed on the dotted line.

CHAPTER 2

DEFINING OUR GOALS

I had dreamed of peaceful pastures and goats grazing contentedly with kids by their sides. Now that we had the land, could we make the dream come true?

By the time we bought our place, we actually had been looking for land for about 14 years. We had experienced three long distance moves during that time, so, after each, we started our search afresh in our new location. It wasn't until the last time that I began to use the internet to look for real estate. As I scoured real estate listings, I also discovered websites and articles about people buying land and what they were doing with it. As I read, I realized that terminology had changed since my early, college days experience. Folks no longer went "back-to-the-land," and became "self-sufficient." Now, they "homesteaded" and became "self-sustaining". They no longer simply lived without electricity, now they made their own and lived "off-grid."

One of the terms that popped up in association with all this was "hobby farm". I found a number of useful articles at Hobbyfarms.com,

Although we had no barn, we figured we could make do with our outbuildings. This one had a carport on the left, an apparent workshop in the middle, and coal storage on the right, still containing lumps of coal, once used to heat the house.

and read them with great interest. The more I read, however, the more I sensed that the type of farming they discussed wasn't what we had in mind. The term "hobby" denotes a recreational activity to which one devotes one's extra time and resources for fun and relaxation. It's what people do for enjoyment apart from the routine of their lives. If they can make a little money at it, that's a plus, but not a necessity. To paraphrase the dictionary, a hobby is an activity or interest pursued for pleasure and not as a main occupation. My spinning, knitting, and weaving fall into that category, as does Dan's pyrography. Wikipedia.com defined hobby farm as a "small farm that is maintained without expectation of being a primary source of income... to provide some recreational land... for sideline income, or are run at an ongoing loss as a lifestyle choice by people with the means to do so."[1] As such, the hobby farmer never becomes self-sufficient, but remains a perpetual consumer to support his or her hobby.

Well, that wasn't us. We weren't looking to farm as a recreational pursuit or an enjoyable sideline. When it came to our land, our home, and what we wanted to do, it wasn't going to be something at which we simply played, it was going to be our life.

The other kind of farming I would call "career farming." That concept tied into another question we had: What exactly were we going to do with our land? Did we want to make our living from it?

The simple answer was yes, but the process of becoming farmers was not so simple. The charming image of an old farmhouse, cows chewing their cuds in a big red barn, chickens pecking amongst the daisies, and kittens in the hayloft, has been steadily swallowed up by industry. Farming is no longer about living in the country, growing crops and livestock, and selling the surplus to help feed folks. Modern farming has become big business. It's about production, profits, and consumerism; it's about science rather than nature. Smaller family farms still exist, but the majority of them struggle. High land and equipment prices keep them in debt. Demands from the food industry dictate what they can grow and how to grow it. Many a farmer must have a second job away from the farm to make ends meet. That wasn't what Dan and I wanted.

Although there were obstacles, we still entertained the idea of becoming career farmers. Besides not having the start-up capital, our biggest problem was that we had no experience in farming. We had bits and pieces of knowledge and a desire to learn, but at the time we knew of no modern day farming apprenticeships. There were workshops, courses, and seminars around the country, but that didn't seem a practical way to learn. College would mean a course of study focusing on industrialized business farming, so that was out of the question.

Another problem is that neither Dan nor I have a business mindset. We're artists who tend to gravitate toward creating and producing, rather than marketing and selling. In the past when we've looked into having our own crafts business, it was the bookkeeping, marketing, sales tax, business and self-employment taxes, etc., that disheartened us. Add to that, the increasing government regulations imposed on small farms: permits, certifications, fees, inspections, etc. As much as we wanted to make our living from our land, this is something else with which we'd have to deal, and we had to ask ourselves how this fit in with simplifying our lives.

Lastly was the question, did we have enough land? We had just bought five acres, about half cleared, the other half wooded with mature pines and scattered hardwoods. It seemed to me that all of our land would have to be dedicated to production in order to make a living at farming. I wondered if we would have enough land for that plus other things we wanted to do with it for personal use.

These are the things we pondered at first. In doing so, I considered another term that popped up frequently in my internet searching:

A view of our outbuildings from the woods. Initially, our wooded area seemed promising as a source for firewood; we could see a number of oaks along the edge of the field. A closer inspection was disappointing; the woods were mostly pine trees.

"homestead". I had pretty much thought of farms and homesteads as different phases of the same thing. After all, isn't that what 18th and 19th century settlers did, turned homesteads into farms? As I read, however, I could see that these terms were now being used in different contexts. To clarify for myself, I looked up a couple more definitions. The following are my words, based on various sources:

• Farm - area of land and structures maintained as a business through producing food, fiber, and fuel. It involves the production and sale of such products for the purpose of making a living.

• Homestead - area of land (rural or urban) and home maintained for the purposes of a simplified, sustainable, self-sufficient lifestyle.

These alone told me that what we were really interested in was homesteading. Not that we ruled out making a living from our land as farmers, but that would be an extension of our goals, not the goal itself. As modern day homesteaders we could utilize the land on a smaller scale to meet most of our own needs. The key words there were *simplified*, *sustainable*, and *self-sufficient*.

Simplified. Although the concept of simplified seems fairly obvious to me, I've been surprised when the term, "simple life," has been interpreted to mean "leisurely life". Granted, "simple" does have many definitions, as any dictionary will show: easy to understand, not elaborate, not ornate, not complicated, free of deceit, common, ordinary, humble, lowly, plain, rudimentary, ignorant, mentally deficient, unsophisticated, naive.

While some of us might find an uncomplicated life appealing, it's doubtful that very many of us would think the same of an ignorant life. We might like to think of ourselves as straightforward and free of deceit, but probably wouldn't care to be referred to as naive, unsophisticated, or mentally deficient. Yet all of these can be meanings of the word "simple."

Its application to one's life will be determined to a great extent by the context of one's lifestyle. A simple life for some may mean dating only one person instead of three. For someone else, simple might mean "easy," as in having a job where one doesn't have to work too hard. Or it might mean not having to spend too many hours in rush hour traffic each day.

For Dan and me, a simplified life is a life not complicated by the pressure of being, doing, or having whatever the latest social trends dictate. We do not want to be slaves to our jobs, nor to accumulate as much money, material wealth, and financial security as we possibly can, nor have as much leisure and "fun" as we can get. In a nutshell, it isn't that we seek to "do nothing;" rather we refuse to compete in the rat race of life.

We want a less hectic life, one that lets us be involved with the natural processes of life; one that relies less on consumerism and more on our relationship with our land. We want a life that keeps us in touch with the natural creation and its gifts.

Sustainable. Like "homesteading," this was another new word for me and it popped up frequently on the internet. The back-to-land movement had promoted self-sufficiency. Was sustainability the same thing?

Technically, no. Sustainability requires that we not use up what we have to the point where there is no more. Of some things, there is a finite quantity, such as fossil fuels. These are not considered sustainable because we can't make more on demand. Eventually we will exhaust them. Wind and solar power, on the other hand, are considered sustainable (or renewable) energy sources, because they are ever present. A resource like wood can be sustainable over the generations if one manages a woodlot wisely and plants a tree for every one cut down.

In addition to substances, sustainability can be applied to practices, such as economics, or how we grow food. Modern industrialized agriculture, which relies heavily on hybridized or genetically modified seed and petroleum-based chemicals (fertilizers, insecticides, and herbicides), is not sustainable because the seeds cannot reproduce themselves and the chemicals must continually be manufactured and applied. This system requires constant input from outside sources, with an end result that it can sustain neither itself nor the land. Permaculture and other organic agricultural methods are sustainable because manufactured inputs are not required and the land is nurtured and improved.

In regards to homesteading, there is a great deal we can do to be sustainable: growing and saving our own seeds, raising our own animals, and making our own electricity. Each one of these would give us the sense of freedom we longed for and enable us to meet our ultimate goal of being self-sufficient.

Self-sufficient. Initially I thought of self-sufficiency as being the same as self-sustaining. I realize now that this isn't necessarily the case. A self-sufficient life will be self-sustaining, but not necessarily the other way around. I can be self-sustaining in particular areas of my life - food or energy for example - but still be dependent on the other providers for everything else. I could be a consumer in a self-sustaining system, such as electricity, without being self-sustaining myself.

Some folks will be quick to point out that complete self-sufficiency is impossible to attain. They are correct. I can't produce my own salt, for example, or toilet paper, though, dare I mention it, there are a dedicated few who use washable rags for that purpose. Because no one can be totally sufficient unto themselves, the term "self-sufficient" often draws criticism as a life goal. Within the context of our personal goals, however, self-sufficiency means not being eternally dependent upon the consumer economic system to meet all of our needs. It means learning to rely more on ourselves, on our willingness to work, learn, and adapt, on our ability to problem solve, and on our lifestyle choices. It means relying less on external resources, especially those that must be purchased in order to live. It means taking responsibility for our choices and not expecting others to fix our mistakes or bail us out. To better clarify what we're about, I have more recently thought the term "self-reliant" to be a better choice.

Either way, the reality of this goal is actually two-fold: we either must be able to produce for ourselves, or learn to live without. In this regard, "simplified" is a good bedfellow to "self-sufficient". For example, when folks begin to consider making their own electricity, one of the first

Our new property had two clearings: one had been kept mowed by a neighbor, the other was mowed only along the property line and was badly overgrown.

questions is: How much do we need? Initially, we may look to our past electric bills to figure that out. We calculate an average or a range, and begin to price systems to meet those needs. For those of us with limited finances, the price tags are quite discouraging. Once the sticker shock wears off, we ask ourselves, do I really need that much electricity? Is it possible to get by with less? Do I really need to run the dishwasher, the clothes dryer, the vacuum cleaner, the computer, and the stereo all at the same time? Do I even need a dishwasher, clothes dryer, vacuum cleaner, computer, and stereo? Having less gadgets and doing more by hand begins to make sense, as does learning how to ration energy.

For Dan and me, energy self-sufficiency is still a future goal. More doable and immediate was beginning to produce our own food. Although we didn't realize it in our goal setting stage, this was going to require simplifying something else - our diet.

Although we'd always had a garden, we, like most folks, were used to buying our food from grocery stores, where we could get anything we wanted, whenever we wanted. We could have tomatoes, grapefruit, and eggs all year long. Or chocolate, brown rice, and bananas. Initially, I had dreams of an exotic summer garden, vast orchards, and a greenhouse where I could keep dwarf coffee, banana, and lemon trees, and a few wintered over tomato plants, all providing us with their fruits all year long. In fact, I bought a Meyers lemon tree right before we moved to the homestead. It took only one winter of having no good place to keep it in the house, to begin to rethink our diet. Not that I'd given up on either lemons or a greenhouse; there was just too much else to do first.

About this time, the local food movement came into my awareness, and I read Barbara Kingsolver's book, *Animal, Vegetable, Miracle*. I began to realize that if my goal is to produce all of my own food, then I am faced with the choice of either trying to grow everything we like to eat, or simplifying our diet by eating only what we can grow. I started to consider what we could grow and grow well in our part of the world. Some things required more work to coax along than others. Some things didn't mind our hot summers with their annual dry spell. I started to think about this as I prepared meals and began to use more of the foods we had the potential to provide for ourselves.

To those three terms, *simplified, sustainable*, and *self-sufficient*, I would add another "S" word that helped shape our goals - *stewardship*. Not a trendy term like "sustainable", it nonetheless summarizes our philosophy toward land. While conservation is the term commonly used in regards to land usage, stewardship evokes a sense of responsibility we feel is important. It implies the supervision or management of something entrusted to one's care. It implies not only responsibility, but also accountability. We believe that one day, we will be accountable for how we lived our lives and for what we did with the things in our possession. Conservation, on the other hand, has come to imply the right to control. Unfortunately this can be tainted with personal or political motives to the detriment of the thing being conserved, as well as those for whom it is conserved. These are small differences that have big implications in regards to how we ultimately view our relationship with the earth.

Some yard cleanup was needed, but not much.

Understanding what we wanted from our land and defining how we would go about it was an important first step. In fact, it was crucial in helping us define our primary goal of working toward self-reliance. This, in turn, continues to give us direction and helps us set our priorities and evaluate choices as they present themselves.

Long term, this goal means something else to us as well. While getting started is costly, over the years we will cut expenses as we do and provide more for ourselves. This means we'll need to buy less. Having fewer expenses means we'll need less money, which means we can decrease the amount of income we must make.

I used to want to think, "What else do we need to do to become self-sufficient?" After our first several years here, I changed that. Now I think, "If the bottom fell out tomorrow, how well could we meet our own needs? What would be the next thing we'd wish we had done?" Not that I'm predicting the bottom is going to fall out tomorrow, but the question does help us prioritize our goals. For our age and income bracket, this makes sense on several levels. While we have no plans of retiring to a life of ease and leisure, neither do we have confidence in retirement investments and social security. We're middle-aged empty-nesters now. As the economy gets worse due to government irresponsibility and corporate corruption, we doubt there will be anything there for us when our time comes to need it. By decreasing our living expenses, we think we have a better chance for, at least, a comfortable lifestyle with purpose, though not an affluent one with leisure.

We are able to think this way partly because of the way we view money. To us, money is a tool, not a source of security. That kind of security is in our land and what we can produce from it. The value of money rises, falls, and sometimes disappears. We will always need money to pay taxes and buy certain items, but the less we need to spend, the less income we need to make for ourselves. And that means more time on the homestead, which is what we set out to do in the first place.

We live in a world governed by an economic system that is based on ever-increasing profit and debt. To us, that seems perilous and doomed to fail. Thanks to the internet, I realized that we weren't the only ones who recognized this. The homesteading movement was alive and well, and we were about to jump on board.

NOTES

[1] "Hobby Farm", *Wikipedia, The Free Encyclopedia*, 21 Nov. 2009. Web, 31 Aug. 2013 <https://en.wikipedia.org/wiki/Hobby_farm>

Chapter 3

Setting Priorities

Our first order of business was to evaluate house and land, and to set priorities.

Our new homestead had been vacant and neglected for a number of years. The house was livable but badly in need of updates and repair: the roof shingles were curling, the old oil furnace smelled like.... well, old oil. The fireplace was stuffed with 1980s newspapers, all the appliances were on their last legs, and the cheap vinyl siding only covered part of the rotting exterior wood siding. We also discovered that it still had some of the original knob and tube wiring, and that the septic tank hadn't been pumped out in who knows how many years. Once all that sunk in, it was overwhelming. But this was the trade-off we'd made with ourselves: a lower, affordable mortgage if we bought a house that needed repair.

The yard and land were overgrown with poison ivy, blackberries, wild roses, saw briars, kudzu, and sapling trees, all of which threatened to take over. There was no fencing and no barn, but there were several old outbuildings, all having seen better days.

The roof was badly worn and we wanted to replace it with a metal roof. We found a DIY metal roofing company and began estimating materials. Then deadlines from our homeowners insurance company pushed us in another direction.

In spite of all this, we were excited and full of plans and ideas. I think if we were younger when we started, we might have prioritized differently. I think we would have done well to focus on the house first, perhaps with a small garden, and then tackled fencing, livestock, outbuildings, more extensive food production, and later, water and energy self-sufficiency. As it was, the younger half of our lives was behind us and we didn't feel we had the time to gradually build our homestead.

Two things pressured us: our middle age was looking to give way to old age, and the world seemed to be falling apart around us. The economy was uncertain, and the recovery for which people hoped seemed dubious. While the government tinkered around in an attempt to find the right economic formula, it became increasingly apparent that integrity had been replaced by greed, in both government and business. In fact, big business, with its insatiable appetite for ever increasing profits, seemed to have direct influence over government laws and policies. Everything coming out of Washington seemed to favor large corporations and their investments, rather than the average citizen. Even the pretense of political party differences was beginning to grow thin.

This related directly to our second concern, retirement. We are just lower middle class folks with no means to buy our way into the investment system. Neither do we have confidence in retirement accounts, social security, medicare, nor government-subsidized health care. In fact, because of these things we could only see our economic situation getting worse. Consequently, we felt impatient to get things done, to get to a place where we felt we could make it on our own if the need arose.

Our motives for homesteading are not noble ones. We aren't trying to save the earth, help stop climate change, or reduce our carbon footprint. Our motives are more personal and more spiritual, and it was from these that we set our priorities. We focused on two practical areas that needed addressing: the house and the land. Both would require a lot of work. We weren't interested in making our nearly 90 year old house a showpiece, but we did need for it to be sturdy, sound, and suited to our needs. Then there

With a house nearly 90 years old, we expected structural problems and were not disappointed. Many problems, like the rotted rim joist under a kitchen window, shown above, were hidden until we began tearing into walls and floors. For a before photo, see page 13. An after photo can be found on page 51.

was the land. It had potential - some was cleared, some wooded, we had some outbuildings - but it needed fencing, nurturing, and a plan to make it productive.

We made settlement on the house the last day of April and moved in around the third week of May, after weeks of cleaning and scrubbing. Dan favored getting started on the house, while I was anxious to get a garden in the ground. He tilled a small plot in the yard for me to plant a garden, and then got started on the first house project: tearing down the old fireplace and chimney, and installing an expensive, EPA approved wood heat stove that we bought at a spring clearance sale.

We wanted to get that stove in before winter, but we also wanted to work outside. The problem was knowing exactly where to begin. While we chiseled bricks and piled them in the yard, we talked. What did we want to do and how did we want to do it? When did we want to do it? Repairing and upgrading the house was important, but so was the land, as it was rapidly being reclaimed by mother nature. What exactly did we want to do with it? Where would we put chickens? Did we want goats or a cow? We could use goats to help clear brush, but what about fencing? Goats need

Summer of 2009 we chose an area for a small garden next to the house. The garden was late going in, but we still got a respectable harvest of summer vegetables.

During our first year, we observed. Mostly, the land had good drainage, but some areas flooded after heavy rains. We also observed seasonal sun and wind patterns.

good fencing. What about bees? A bigger garden? We would need to grow grain and hay if we had livestock. What about an orchard? Fruit trees should be planted this year, preferably in the autumn to give them a good start, but where?

Once the excitement settled, the amount of work that needed to be done was overwhelming. It was all too easy to become distracted with details, such as the style of chicken coop we wanted or what breed of goats we should get. The thing that helped the most was continually keeping our primary goal in mind, that of becoming as self-sufficient as we are able. In the beginning, the kind of chicken coop or breed of goats wasn't important. What was important was determining the steps we would need to get there.

The company that carried our homeowners insurance policy dictated our priorities somewhat. Under threat of canceling our policy, they insisted on things such as a new handrail for the back porch steps, and a new roof. Even so, we knew focusing on the house first was the best plan, because it would give us time to assess our land in regards to sun, wind, weather, drainage, and seasonal patterns.

In assessing the house, it quickly became obvious that it needed structural repairs. It also needed to facilitate our lifestyle as our center of operations. The kitchen, for example, needed to be a workshop that could accommodate not only food preparation, but food preservation, milk processing, cheese making, etc. This became a priority because we can live without electricity, if need be, but we can't live without food.

One thing we didn't want to do was to get ahead of ourselves, even though the order of some projects seemed logical. For example, we needed to put up fences before we could get animals. Deciding exactly where those fences should go would take more planning, and would hinge on other things, such as where we would put the garden and where we would build a barn. Dan thought we needed to map it out, like the Blake place in Eric Sloane's *Diary of an Early American Boy*.[1] We needed a visual diagram that would keep our goals before us. It would be from this that we could set priorities while keeping the big picture in mind. By knowing what we wanted our homestead to look like, there would be less chance of arbitrarily choosing a location for something we'd later have to move. Developing a master plan became our next step.

Notes
[1] Eric Sloane, *Diary of an Early American Boy* (Mineola, NY: Dover Publications, 2004) x – xiii.

CHAPTER 4

DEVELOPING A MASTER PLAN

Our master plan is a diagram of what we want our homestead to look like when it grows up. It is a sketch that puts all the pieces together and helps us visualize the fulfillment of our dream and goals. It helps us in our decision making and as we set our priorities. It serves as a visual reminder of what's been decided so far, because ideas fly and so does one's memory. By having a master plan, we can better determine how each step fits into the big picture.

Our master plan has undergone a revision each year. Each year, we become more acquainted with our land and the nuances of our regional climate. From experience, we learn what works for us and what doesn't. As we research, we come across information and materials from those who have forged ahead, with means and methods compatible with our goals: Gene Logsdon, Joel Salatin, and Sepp Holzer, to name a few.

Our property is pie shaped, as you can see from an old aerial photo.

A topographical map shows our land as a series of ridges sloping down toward the back of the property. The house is on the highest point, excellent for good drainage.

This, plus the lay of the land, presents certain challenges that shape how we map things out. Our first master plan focused only on the cleared areas. We drew it in August, 2009, after much discussion.

To start, we had the house, carport, and two outbuildings. We also had quite a few pecan trees, several fig trees, and a rabbiteye blueberry bush. By the time we drew that first master plan, we had planted the hedgerow, a privacy hedge of four-foot Leyland Cypresses, along the road. Everything else was what we hoped to accomplish: barn, root cellar, chicken yard, fencing, pond, herb and vegetable gardens, plus more fruit and shade trees.

Some things were more definite than others. The garden and pasture were things we were certain about. The pond less so, although the dish-like contour of the land seemed to suggest it.

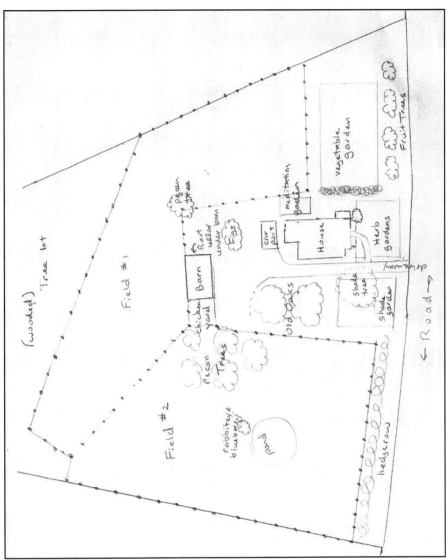

Sketch of our first Master Plan, August 2009. I traced the outline of the property and buildings from our survey map. Placement of everything else is approximate, but it give us a rough visual of what we're working toward as we plan projects.

Admittedly, the placement of the fences looks odd on this two dimensional drawing, but the proposed fence followed the contour of the land, a series of ridges descending toward the back of the property. In fact, we found remnants of old, rusted fencing in the same places we proposed to put our fences, giving us a sense that, just maybe, we were on the right track.

Some things on the plan, such as the fig trees and blueberry bush, we did not know about initially. I discovered the fig trees while clearing out the thick overgrown brush. A neighbor told us about the blueberry bush, also hidden in bushes and trees.

That first year we worked hard. We not only planted the Leyland Cypresses, but also our first fruit trees: apples, pears, peaches, and elderberry bushes. Dan tilled the ground for the large vegetable garden, an 80 foot by 60 foot plot based on the "Grow N' Store" garden from Dick Raymond's book, *The Joy of Gardening*. We had the soil tested by our state cooperative extension service, and added what they recommended.

Another project was to modify our outbuildings. In one, we made a storage area for garden and yard tools. The other, we converted into a small "barn." We decided to use the left side for chickens, the right for a few goats, and the middle for feed, storage, and a milking stand.

After we completed the "barn," we started fencing the field for goats. We had never put up a fence before, so I stood there with library book in hand, reading what to do next while Dan did it. It was awkward at first, but as we gained experience we picked up momentum.

The building we called "the coal barn" had a lean-to that became a garden shed for storing our riding lawn mower, wheelbarrow, and all our garden hand tools.

This 10 foot by 27 foot outbuilding was to become our "barn."

We added the gate on the right to create a goat stall. The middle door gives access to a chicken coop on the left, as well as feed storage and milking area in-between.

Above: We fenced in a chicken yard on the backside of the building. The ramp was necessary because of the building's diagonal bracing at the interior corners. Below: We set the first fence posts for the goat field at the front of the shed.

Six months later, we were ready to do some fine tuning to our master plan. Our first revision was very similar to the original, but included the improvements we'd already made, as well as other things we'd begun to think about, such as where to put a greenhouse and installing a rainwater catchment system.

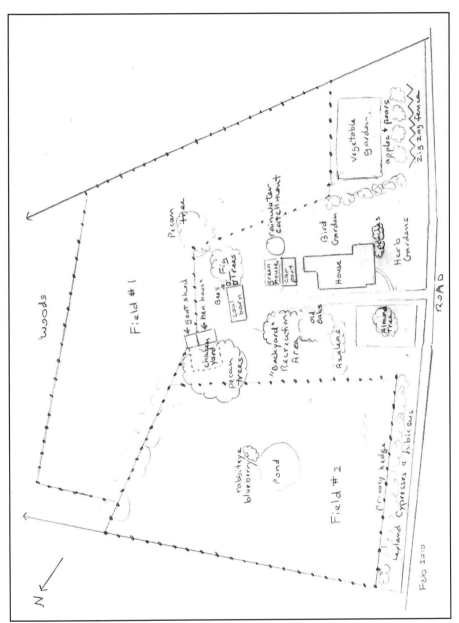

Revised Master Plan, February 2010

The fruit and shade trees were now planted and could be labeled according to their specific types. We were rethinking placement of a future barn, and so, on this revision, I left the outbuildings as they are. We defined an outdoor recreational area for ourselves, labeled "backyard" on the plan. It was shaded by three huge, old oak trees and was where we'd have an occasional campfire. It would be a good place to build a permanent charcoal/wood grill, outdoor oven, and put a picnic table. It would require a privacy fence though, since we had a neighbor in direct view across the street. I transplanted azalea bushes there in hopes of growing those for privacy. In addition, we had just gotten our first baby chicks and goats were imminent too. We were definitely making progress.

Other things popped up along way, things that weren't on our master plan, yet, or things that changed as we began to think them through. One of these was where we would grow grain and other field crops.

Since one of our primary goals is to be food self-sufficient, we needed to grow grain to feed us and our animals, too. Where to put a grain field was one question, but, also, how much would we need for a year's supply and how much land would it take? We didn't know how to answer those questions, and, finally, decided to just make a start, see what we got, and adjust from there. Of more immediate concern was more fencing. Grain would have to be fenced to keep the goats out.

Our first baby chicks arrived Feb. 2010, a straight run mix of four heritage breeds.

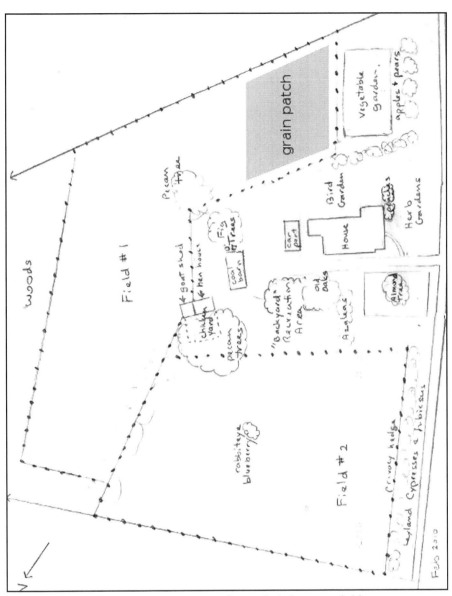

Amended 2010 Master Plan included a grain field.

After much deliberation, we amended our master plan to include a grain field. It had the potential for irrigation and would be fairly easy to fence. The plan was to plant corn there, the following summer.

In May of 2011, we purchased our first two bucks, to breed our does. We had fenced off part of our big pasture for them and built a log buck barn, dubbed "Fort William".

Our buck barn was constructed of downed pine trees from our woods. Standing in the doorway are our two Pygmy bucks, 8 week old Chipper & 4 year old McGruff (aka Gruffy). The barn was later chinked and hinged window covers were added.

By July, it was time for another revision of the master plan. The grain field, buck pasture, and buck barn needed to be added, as well as the fruit and nut trees I had planted. We also had ideas for fencing part of the woods for the goats, and a possible location for future pigs too.

This was the first plan to expand into our wooded area. On our first master plan we labeled it "tree lot," hoping it would provide our firewood. Good firewood, however, is hardwood, and our hardwoods were mostly saplings. The mature trees were pine, which are too soft and too resinous to produce good heat. Because of its high water content, burning pine causes the resin to build up in the chimney as creosote, which easily catches fire. All that meant we needed another plan for our woods.

The other thing that grew in the woods was kudzu. Invading from a neighbor's field, it threatened to engulf our woods and strangle out our trees. Goats would help keep it at bay, plus, benefit from eating all the "browse" of leaves, shrubs, and brush.

Once again, we revised the location for a barn. The pond idea wasn't entirely abandoned, but seemed less a priority and so didn't make it onto this version of the master plan. It seemed, though, that we finally had it all together.

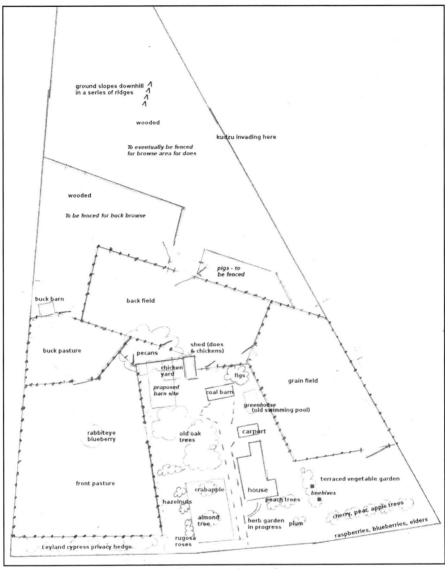

ground slopes downhill
in a series of ridges

wooded

kudzu invading here

*To eventually be fenced
for browse area for does*

wooded

To be fenced for buck browse

pigs - to
be fenced

buck barn

back field

buck pasture

pecans

shed (does
& chickens)

chicken
yard

figs

grain field

*proposed
barn site*

coal barn

greenhouse
(old swimming pool)

rabbiteye
blueberry

old oak
trees

carport

terraced vegetable garden

beehives

front pasture

crabapple

house

hazelnuts

peach trees

almond
tree

cherry, pear, apple trees

herb garden
in progress

plum

raspberries, blueberries, elders

rugosa
roses

Leyland cypress privacy hedge

Revised Master Plan, July 2011

Although the 2011 plan seemed pretty settled, we began to rethink where we should grow grain. We had struggled for two summers with established perennial vines and weeds growing in the grain field, and it seemed to be a losing battle. After reading *Sepp Holzer's Permaculture* and Joel Salatin's *You Can Farm*, it made more sense to follow their examples and utilize pigs to root these out and till the soil for us. Dan suggested we put our first pigs in the weedy grain field, and plant field crops elsewhere. This seemed like a smarter idea with less work involved for us.

In August 2012 we revised our Master Plan again. It updates our pig area and adds another browse area in the woods for the goats. We updated our ideas for a few other things as well: barns, greenhouse, privacy fences, and subdividing our front pasture. This master plan is the current plan in effect, although it, too, is subject to future revisions.

August 2012 Master Plan, revised January 2013.

The barn and outbuildings have been much discussed over the years as we've tried to visualize our various ideas for a barn. We've discussed size, function, and location. Because of cost we've considered improving our existing outbuildings, rather than build one big, new barn.

The privacy fences on the plan were added to the master plan because our chickens, in particular, make our property a dog magnet. Also, we

The tell-tale signs of an old swimming pool were hidden by brush. We might not have known what it was if it hadn't been for neighbors. The current plan is to use it as the foundation for a greenhouse with, hopefully, a root cellar.

Our first privacy fence helps define our backyard and doubles as a place to stack firewood. A second privacy fence is planned along the front pasture property line, to block the view from chicken chasing dogs and fence-climbing children.

hope to build a greenhouse someday, perhaps utilizing the old in-ground swimming pool as a foundation, if it is sound enough. We learned about it from neighbors who recalled swimming in it as children. It had been filled in years before and was badly overgrown with shrubs and vines by the time we bought the place.

The beauty of having a master plan is that it gives structure to our decision making. It is a visual representation of how we want to use the land and what will go where. When we prioritize projects, we have a better sense of how they will affect everything else. Our master plan is by no means written in stone, and as you saw, we adapt it readily. For those reasons, it is probably one of the most useful tools we have.

CHAPTER 5

THE ESTABLISHMENT PHASE

Structural repairs and upgrades to the house are part of establishing a functioning homestead. Most of these we've done ourselves. A few jobs, such as having the new roof put on, we hired out. We discovered that the original roof was a shake roof.

I like to call our beginning years of homesteading "the establishment phase." We have our land and the goal of becoming self-reliant, but it's going to take a lot get there: knowledge, equipment, tools, resources, and time. Because it is just the two of us, it is especially going to take time.

We are actually still in the establishment phase because although we have accomplished a lot, we still have a long way to go. In four and a half years, we've built fences, planted fruit and nut trees, established a large vegetable garden and a quarter acre grain field. We've gotten chickens, goats, and guinea fowl. We've done a lot of work on the house: made much needed repairs to roof and structure, installed a wood heater and wood cookstove, completely overhauled the kitchen, turned the back porch into a summer and canning kitchen, started upgrading windows and insulating walls, upgraded wiring, upgraded plumbing with water conservation systems in mind, installed a rainwater catchment system, and started replacing the deteriorating exterior siding.

While we can look back and be encouraged by our progress, the unfortunate reality is that it is expensive to build and establish a self-sustaining homestead. Land is expensive, building is expensive, fencing is expensive, equipment is expensive, animals are expensive, feeding them is expensive, alternative energy systems are expensive. Any savings we might realize from having a garden for vegetables, chickens for eggs, and goats for milk, is quickly swallowed up by the next thing on the project list.

In the beginning, of course, buying what we need is a necessity, since very few of us inherit the family farm. We need knowledge, resources, tools, and equipment to achieve a self-sufficient life. The danger here is the potential to become nothing more than hobby homesteaders in the end, always in route and never arriving, always buying and never learning to live within the means of what we can provide and do for ourselves.

I have gradually come to realize that there are two aspects to establishing one's homestead. One is the mental/emotional part, the other is a practical/material part. Initially, both of these are largely formed by our culture, or perhaps our reaction to it. They are shaped by it and what we perceive as its faults. They determine the expectations of what we want our homestead to look like and how we are going to set about accomplishing it.

The mental/emotional part is the source of our enthusiasm and motivation. It's what gets us started and becomes the basis for the expectations of what we want our homestead to become. For Dan and me, there were several components to this. One was a basic dissatisfaction with the typical American lifestyle. The endless cycle of work > spend > buy > want more > work > etc., wasn't fulfilling; in fact, it was frustrating. The great American goal of leisure and fun was empty. Our own entertainment consisted, in part, of reading books written by authors who lived in the late 19th and early 20th centuries. True, they had less, but they wanted less. There was a basic contentment and satisfaction with life that is missing in society today. We began to understand that there is another way to live. This way is connected to a relationship with the land and the sense of purpose that comes from being dependent on it, instead of being dependent on others.

Ten day old guinea fowl keets. We got them for tick control after losing one of our dogs to Lymes disease. Guineas are said to be excellent foragers and insect eaters.

The practical/material part follows the mental/emotional. It, too, is influenced by our culture, a culture that has trained us to be consumers rather than doers for ourselves. Because of that, the only way we know to accomplish the fulfillment of our dream of self-sufficiency is to buy everything we need to make it happen. The very thing from which we want to get away is the only means of getting there.

Now, unless we inherit that proverbial family farm, it is true that most of us, indeed, have to buy what we need to get established. Not only do we have to buy the place, but we have to buy building materials, fencing, animals, garden seeds and tools, equipment, etc. The problem, however, is that we rarely know instinctively how to be frugal, how to get by with what's at hand, how to wait, how to make do, how to do without, or how to discern our needs from our wants. We assume we need certain things, or have to do things a certain way, because that's how it's done. Because we lack the know-how and skills, we turn to the experts. I know I did. But what I didn't understand was that the experts don't always have the same goals we do.

The eye-opener for me was chickens. I had read my chicken raising books and taken good notes about raising and keeping chickens. I felt like I had a handle on everything except, perhaps, feed. I couldn't imagine being able to feed my chickens myself, considering the long list of ingredients that went into properly formulated chicken feed. Some of them weren't even available locally (fish meal?), and I wasn't going to mail order anything to feed chickens, so I bought commercial feed.

My books also claimed that hens stop laying during winter's short daylight hours, and that egg production drops rapidly the second year. The advice was to keep a light bulb burning in the hen house all winter, and that it makes economical sense to replace one's entire flock every spring. Dan is very much against artificial methods of any sort when it comes to animals, including egg laying, so we didn't use that light bulb. While egg production decreased during moulting and when the days were short of daylight, my hens still gave me about half the number of eggs I'd gotten all summer. Then, (probably because they didn't read the same book), they continued to lay their second and third years the same as the first. As I reread my chicken books, I realized that the authors' goals were different from mine. My goals were to have enough eggs to meet our needs, enough chickens to eat a chicken dinner on occasion, and to perpetuate my flock. The book was about profit and production. Even their breeds were different. In the end, I realized their means and methods didn't necessarily apply to me. Their system didn't help me meet my goals.

Another example was the realization that we were subconsciously trying to achieve a certain "look" about the place. We didn't want it to look like a dump, but on the other hand, "picturesque" takes time, money, and energy away from truly needful things. I often resented having neighbors so close, because it made me feel obligated to mow the front yard. If we had been more rural, I wouldn't have worried about how the front yard looked, and would have spent that time establishing an extensive permaculture herb garden to replace the lawn. I still mow the lawn out of respect for my neighbors, but I've learned to worry less about the overall impression that our work-in-progress presents to the passer-by. Instead we are working on making upgrades and repairs that will aid us in our quest toward self-sufficiency. At first, that means focusing on our home's interior; a more aesthetic exterior will happen in time.

Hopefully, during the establishment phase, there is an adaptation, an adjustment from the ideal dream homestead to what we can do realistically. This is not a one-size-fits-all adjustment, but is based on one's land, climate, and resources. And one's goals. While the basics are absolutely necessary (food, water, shelter), we realized we don't actually "need" everything we thought we did. We need a winter food supply, but don't actually need a greenhouse in our climate, for example. If I want fresh produce, I can learn winter gardening and storage techniques. I adapt to my chickens by using less eggs. We can eat what's available at that time of year. We did feel that a good reference library was essential, and certain equipment. I can't put up my tomatoes without jars, lids, and a canner.

Extensive projects such as the kitchen had to be done in stages. Pictured is the kitchen entry way and dining alcove.

Upper left: Before, as it was originally. Upper right: To replace the load bearing post in the middle of the room, Dan milled a new beam and two posts from one of the pine trees on the property. Lower left: When we rebuilt the water damaged wall, we installed a salvaged energy efficient window. Lower right: After.

The kitchen has been the most challenging room so far. I wanted an efficient food preparation and processing workshop that was convenient and pleasant to work in.

Some things, though, we began to rethink. Do I really need one of those cute, barn-like chicken coops where I can collect eggs by standing outside and lifting a lid? Or would a partition in the old shed do, with nest boxes built of recycled materials we had lying around? Do I really need to buy the materials to build raised beds in the garden and then buy soil to fill them? Or could I simply mark the beds on the ground and work to gradually improve the soil, building bed borders as time and resources become available?

These are the kinds of adjustments that were made as we began to evaluate our goals, time, and financial resources. We had a dream, but as we learned from experience we began to adjust our goals and expectations.

One thing I've noticed is that as the homesteading movement grows, so does homestead marketing. There is profit to be made by selling things to homesteaders: tools, equipment, feeds, bulk foods, seeds, gadgets, ideas, disaster and preparedness kits, online classes, how-tos, and DIY plans. Look, even I'm doing it. I'm writing a book to sell, aren't I?

While the growing availability of such resources is helpful, we gradually became aware that not everyone selling something is doing it

We made nest boxes from discarded cardboard tubes rescued from a dumpster.

because they believe in self-sufficiency or homesteading. Some are sincere, but some are simply targeting a new demographic for its profit potential. As we researched various areas, such as alternative energy and water conservation systems, it became obvious that the "expertise" being offered was all too often a sales pitch geared toward selling a particular product. Even the do-it-yourself articles often fell short. They would give enough information so that we thought we could do it ourselves, but never got to the step-by-step nitty-gritty of the thing.

We also realized that not everything being touted as "green", and carbon efficient is what it appears to be. It may be that of itself, but may require a wasteful, energy intensive process to produce. Pellet stoves come to mind. The concept of recycling wood waste as a heat source is excellent, and while the stoves themselves are energy efficient, the process of making the pellets is not. Then there's the use of fossil fuels to transport the product, as well as keeping the pellet stove owner a perpetual consumer. That is, unless that pellet stove owner wishes to pay thousands of dollars for a machine to make his or her own pellets. It is so easy to get caught up in a partial truth and never think a thing through. It's easy because this is how we were raised, to buy.

For the record, I do not think there is anything wrong with many of the products and ideas on the homesteading market today. Many are clever and useful. My point is, as long as I'm spending money to establish or maintain my homestead, I am not yet self-sufficient.

There is a flip side to all of this, because it is unrealistic to assume that self-sufficiency means one never needs money. In fact, I realize that some people might assume that self-sufficiency is isolationism. This is one reason why I lean toward the term "self-reliant." While we can trade and barter for many things, money still is a reality. It is essential, especially in the beginning, because most of us start our homestead with nothing but a mortgage. Even after we become fairly well established, there are still taxes to pay and things we can't provide for ourselves: salt, baking soda, saw blades, kerosene for the lamps. Some of these we may be able to barter for, some we will not.

Oftentimes, having a home business is part of a homesteader's self-sufficiency formula. The danger here is the potential to become part of the very thing we are trying to escape. We can get caught up in trying to make more and more money, rather than supporting ourselves by offering a truly useful product or service to the community. I realize some folks may not see the difference, but that is just another indicator of how our cultural conditioning has changed our mindset as a people.

The question that must ultimately be answered is, when is enough, enough? There is a quirk of human nature that always thinks, "if only I had .....". Usually the blank is filled in with "more money," but for a homesteader, it can be other things. For us, it's "if only we had a tractor," "if only we had a lumber mill," "if only we had a proper barn," "if only the mortgage was paid off." It's tough because each of these things is good in itself, but it ought to beg the question - when are we finally established as a homestead?

I play a mental game with myself that helps me bring our progress into perspective. It's a "what if" game, based on whatever imaginary emergency or doomsday scenario suits my fancy at the time. What if Dan was suddenly unemployed for months on end? What if, for some reason, civilization as we know it collapsed? How prepared would we be? The answer, at this point, is that we would have shelter, heat, and could eat. We would not have our accustomed diet, but we would have the food and the means to cook it. We wouldn't have electricity for lights at night, but we do have kerosene lanterns. We are on city water, so having that could be questionable. We do have a Berkey water filter, so we have the potential to have clean drinking and cooking water, provided we have a water source.

I do put limits on this game, and do not extend these "what ifs" beyond the evaluation of our immediate ability to meet our own needs.

Stretching welded wire fence with a fence stretcher and come-along. We taught ourselves how to put up fence our first year here. Fencing is an ongoing project.

The sole purpose of this mental exercise is to help prioritize our goals, not to worry about what might happen in the future. It helps me determine whether something is truly a need, or simply a want; if we suddenly had to do without, what's the next thing we would need in order to survive? Would we regret certain purchases or pursuits as unnecessary? Perhaps this seems an extreme way to go about this, but it provides me with endless hours of entertainment when I'm about mundane tasks such as weeding the garden or grinding flour. (I play another version of this game when faced with piles of long neglected housework. I ask myself, "What if company were to drop in unexpectedly right now, what about the house would embarrass me most?" Then I start with that.)

The bottom line is that we must learn to prioritize our needs and make choices that actually help us meet our goals. Buying to meet our needs means we are still consumers and will continue to be for as long as we want or need something that somebody else has. If my goal truly is self-sufficiency, then at some point I'm going to have to learn to be content. I'm going to have to stop wanting more, to stop looking at buying something as the solution to a problem. I'm going to have to get off the consumer mindset merry-go-round. I'm going to have to adjust my expectations to the reality in which we live.

Will we ever actually achieve this? Will we ever get out of the establishment phase and become truly self-reliant? I honestly don't know the answer to that. Truth be told, I doubt it. Not at our age. If we had started in our 20s, 30s, or even 40s, I think we would have had a better chance. Or, if we had a significantly larger income, as ironic as it sounds, then we could buy our way into self-sufficiency. So why do we continue? That one I can answer, and answer without much thought. We continue because the journey is worth it.

CHAPTER 6

FOOD SELF-SUFFICIENCY: FEEDING OURSELVES

Garden, July, 2010. An Italian grape hoe lies on the ground in front.

There are realities to food self-sufficiency that we didn't realize in the beginning. Producing one's own food is often a primary motivator for folks who seek to homestead, and is one of the most important aspects of becoming truly self-reliant. But it doesn't happen overnight, it happens over years. We often need to learn the techniques and skills involved, we need to prepare these areas on our homestead, and some things, like an orchard, take time to grow.

It also didn't take long to figure out that when it comes to food self-sufficiency, we really only have two choices. We must either learn to grow everything we want to eat, or we must learn to eat what we can grow. It didn't take very many failed attempts at trying to grow a particular food to figure that out. Most of us start with a vegetable garden and learn how to preserve our harvest by canning, freezing, dehydrating, root cellaring, and eventually lacto-fermenting. I did. In fact, during our first year on our homestead, I was able to preserve an entire year's worth of vegetables for our use. Fruit trees and bushes are a good next step for homesteaders, and of course animals take it to a whole new level. Trying to grow our own grains has been a new experience altogether.

What Do We Need?

Being the analytical sort, I started my journey toward food self-sufficiency with a list of food categories. I asked myself how we could raise at least something in each of those categories:

- vegetables
- fruits
- starches
- proteins
- sweeteners
- fats
- beverages
- miscellaneous

As I analyzed each of these, I was really analyzing our diet. After several summer gardens, I realized that some things grow better in my area than others. If I wanted to simplify my garden work, I would need to focus mostly on those things and incorporate more of them into our diet. We might love grapefruit for breakfast, but figs, blueberries, peaches, and strawberries are more realistic than trying to keep a dwarf grapefruit tree. I also realized that to be truly food self-sufficient, I need to perpetuate what we want to grow. That meant learning how to save seeds. My thoughts and notes about my food categories turned out something like the following:

Vegetables

Vegetables probably offer the greatest variety to the homesteader's diet. I've grown many vegetable gardens over the years but until we bought this place, I never considered having a self-sustaining vegetable supply. Like every gardener, I love to look at seed catalogs and order seeds. Vegetable self-sufficiency, however, means saving seeds. I had saved seeds in the past, mostly easy things like green beans, sunflowers, and okra. Other things, such as tomato and cucumber seeds, are a little trickier and I had to learn the techniques. Then, too, plants like carrots are biennials and don't produce seed until their second year. On top of that, some things can cross-pollinate, such as different types of squash or corn. This is a problem because the seeds planted from these crosses are hybrids, and hybrids do not reproduce true to the parent plant. I realized I had a lot to learn. To start, I began to purchase only heirloom or open-pollinated (non-hybrid) seeds. My long term goal is to eventually save all my own seed. I try to add to my seed collection each year, saving enough for more than one year's garden in case of crop failure. As I experiment with new vegetables and varieties, I save the ones that we like and do well in our climate.

Besides seed saving, I realized I needed to take advantage of our regional climate and long growing season. That meant a fall garden that extended into a winter harvest. While a root cellar was on my original goal list, I learned that I don't really need one, as long as my root crops get a deep layer of mulch in the fall. I realized that if I could harvest fresh root vegetables all winter long, then we could have fresh garden eating year

Basket of summer vegetables: cucumbers, okra, tomatoes, a pepper, and green beans

around. This was something I had to learn by experimenting and observing. In fact, my seasonal problems were somewhat reversed from more northerly gardeners: many things, even some warm weather crops, do not like our scorching summers with their annual dry spell.

Fruits

These were second on my list. They are usually perennials and take more time to establish: trees, bushes, even strawberries are perennials. Some can be garden grown on a yearly basis, like melons or husk cherries. While I've yet to grow husk cherries, we learned that an overabundance of melons can be dehydrated as a tasty fruit leather-like snack, or frozen to add to fruit smoothies.

We planted our fruit trees that first autumn, choosing dwarfs and semi-dwarfs because they need less space and take less time to mature. The trade-off is that they produce less because they are smaller. We were fortunate that the property had established fig trees and a blueberry bush when we moved here. We also have wild muscadine grapes and a native persimmon tree. Because fruits are mostly perennial, I took less care to get antique or open-pollinated varieties.

Starches

Because of dietary choices, starches have lost popularity in the past several years. Many folks have gone low-carb to lose weight, or perhaps have gluten intolerance, which limits the kinds of starches they can eat. For us, bread is, as they say, "the staff of life," and we felt it was an important addition to our diet. Our breakfasts, for example, are largely cereal based, with yogurt or kefir, and fruit in season.

I considered two categories for starches: vegetable and grain. For us, vegetable starches include corn and potatoes. These grow well here and we like them both. One year I used sweet potatoes as our main starch, because my potato crop didn't do well. We fell in love with oven baked sweet potato fries. Corn can be frozen or canned and used like a vegetable, or dried as a grain to make corn meal or hominy. Other grain possibilities include wheat, oats, barley, spelt, amaranth, quinoa, or anything else at which we want to try our hand.

Our first experiment in growing grain was a small patch of wheat. I prepared a bed in the garden and planted it in the fall for a spring harvest. Harvesting was done with a scythe, but threshing turned out to be very labor intensive, as well as difficult. I tried a handmade flail, a section of old

Our small, experimental wheat patcht. Our grain growing resources were Gene Logsdon's <u>Small-Scale Grain Raising</u> & <u>Homegrown Whole Grains</u> by Sara Pitzer.

garden hose (idea courtesy of Gene Logsdon[1]), a rubber mallet, even a sledge hammer, all in an attempt to separate the grains from the chaff. They stuck like glue. I later realized that they had probably not ripened enough. I confess I was concerned that if we had waited too long to harvest, the heads would shatter and we would lose it to the ground. In the end, most of it was used as chicken feed. Because growing our own animal feeds is also a goal, the experiment was not a total loss and there was no waste; even the straw was used. It did much to broaden my experiential knowledge base, but threshing will still have to be mastered.

I have experimented with other grains as well, including amaranth, corn, and oats. I found grain amaranth easier to thresh than wheat, but too small to winnow. Still, it is easy to grow and harvest, and has value as animal feed. Growing oats is similar to growing wheat, as is the way it's threshed and winnowed. Harvesting and processing corn is the easiest.

Threshing and winnowing are well suited to autumn or winter, when there is less to do in the garden. There are many motorized threshing ideas on YouTube, and making one of these is on our goal list. We also realized

Hand grinding wheat with my Country Living grain mill. The extension on the handle is called a "power bar." It increases torque and makes grinding easier.

that besides needing space to process our grain, we need a place to store it. Our original outbuildings are small and limited for this purpose, so that is a consideration as we work on a design for a future barn.

Proteins

Proteins could be animal or vegetable, and I planned to grow both. In the vegetable category, we could have meals of complementary proteins, such as baked beans and cornbread. The animal protein category is much more diverse, including eggs, dairy products, and meat. All of these were on my list of foods that we can provide for ourselves.

Now, written down like that, the goal of raising our own meat seems pretty straightforward and emotionally sterile. If one is vegetarian, then the question of raising one's own meat is not a question at all. In fact, the topic is likely disagreeable, to say the least. For a meat eater, however, it is a question of no little importance, especially if one's goal is to have a self-sustaining food supply.

There are two options here: taking the animals to a meat processor or doing it oneself. We've done both. In some areas one can hire someone to come out and do the killing and dressing. We don't have that around here so transportation is a consideration if we take the animals to someone else.

Doing it oneself initially makes more sense with smaller animals like chickens or rabbits. For larger animals such as goats, hogs, or even a cow, it's a much bigger job requiring the proper tools and set-up. There is the killing and dressing, then the butchering or cutting up the meat, and finally the clean-up plus disposal of unwanted parts of the carcass. To be technically self-sufficient one would do all of one's own butchering. Whether or not to broaden that to utilizing community resources depends on one's goals. Either way, having the knowledge and skill is invaluable.

If one researches the topic of home killing and butchering on the internet, one discovers it can be extremely controversial. In some ways it seems odd that it should be so. Backyard chickens were once common in our culture, along with backyard gardens, even in urban areas. Butchering chickens was an acceptable culinary skill, practiced by many a housewife. Yet butchering one's own meat is a concept that is largely foreign today, so much so, that it can be a volatile and emotionally charged issue.

Eggs are an important source of protein for us and valuable for leavening baked goods. The two speckled ones were laid by my Welsummer hens.

I think, though, that the reasons for this are less about dietary choices and the rights of animals, and more about how far corporate farming and food industrialization have taken us from the natural world. Our so called advancements have mentally and emotionally sanitized us to the point where most people are no longer in touch with the actual sources of their food, (it comes from the grocery store in tidy packages, right?) or what real food is ("But I like the taste of chemicals," someone once told me). This isn't limited to meat. Many folks are afraid of raw milk and I've known people who refused to eat anything from a garden because it didn't come in a package from a store.

Many people are aware of how far commercial food processing has taken us from quality, nutritious, "real" food, hence the growing movement toward homesteading, home food production, and simpler living. However, simpler doesn't necessarily mean easier. Simple living requires hard work, as well as hard choices. If one wants to eat meat, for example, then what to do about it is one of those choices.

SWEETNERS

My natural sweetener of choice would be maple syrup. Unfortunately, we have no mature maple trees on the property and, considering our age, feel they are too slow-growing to consider planting as a source for sap. Most realistic for us would be honey and sorghum. For honey there would be an investment in bees, hives, and equipment, including a honey extractor, plus containers to store it. For sorghum we'd need a press and a way to boil the juice down to syrup. These were more things to add to my wish list, but we have reasonable expectation that we can do them.

FATS

I had abandoned vegetable oils initially, after reading Sally Fallon's *Nourishing Traditions*. With that, I also abandoned the idea of growing our own sources for homemade vegetable oils. Small, hand-crank oil presses are available, but the amount of work involved seems intense to me. Further research (raypeat.com) convinced me that our best options were the saturated fats many people shunned. For us, two seemed most realistic: butter and lard. Milk from goat breeds like Nubian, Nigerian Dwarf, and Kinder yield a high amount of butterfat which can be made into butter. By raising pigs, we could render our own lard as well as have a meat source. Tallow from cow fat could be a possibility, although we don't have enough land to raise a cow. Neither do we need the amount of milk a dairy cow

Rendering goat fat. The fat is cut into small pieces and melted with enough water to cover the bottom of the cast iron Dutch oven. As the water evaporates, the fat melts. It is strained and poured off into jars. The unmelted bits are the cracklings.

would give, nor have freezer space for a whole beef. Besides pigs (still future), rendering goat fat is currently the best option for us.

BEVERAGES

Besides water, the top of our list here is coffee, although I can't see myself growing a greenhouse full of dwarf coffee trees. Herbal teas are more realistic, and some, like roasted chicory root, are heartier than leaf teas. Most people would consider milk a beverage, although neither Dan nor I are milk drinkers. All our goat milk goes to making yogurt, kefir, and cheese, or feeding other animals. Dogs, cats, chickens, and pigs all love milk and benefit nutritionally. Another possibility is canning fruit and vegetable juices. Something else we like is a soda with our Friday night pizza. Fortunately, there's even a homemade substitutes for this: homebrewed root beer, lacto-fermented juices, teas made with whey, and water kefir. I've never tried the root beer, and have had no success with lacto-fermenting beverages with whey. I can tell you that fruit juice flavored kefir soda is very tasty. Homebrewing of beer and wine is something folks do as well.

Water as a beverage is important here, although I think folks don't always think of it that way. Still, it's the primary component of other beverages we make, such as coffee and tea. Besides that, it is used for cooking and gardening, and the animals drink it too. Considering recent media discussion of the availability (or not) of pure water, it definitely has a place in the consideration of food self-sufficiency. Because of the amount of chlorine in our tap water, we bought a water filter for home use.

MISCELLANEOUS

In this category I considered things such as seasonings, salt, and leavening. Also foods that we use in small amounts such as jams, jellies, pickles, relishes, and nuts. Cracklings would be another example. These items may not be strictly necessary, but they do add flavor and variety to our meals.

I can grow herbs to season our food, but spices such as cinnamon and nutmeg don't seem feasible. Ginger is something that can be successfully grown in a pot. Salt is something we'd have to purchase. Vinegars and pectin can both be made at home, although I haven't tried either yet.

Leavenings can include yeast, baking powder, baking soda mixed with buttermilk or whey, eggs, and sourdough starter. Baking powder can be commercial or homemade. It contains cream of tartar (an acid) and baking soda (an alkali) along corn starch for a buffer. The addition of the corn starch delays the acid and the alkali from neutralizing the baking powder. In the presence of a liquid, a chemical reaction creates carbon dioxide bubbles which causes the rise.[2] One can add the cream of tartar and baking soda at the time of mixing, or use baking soda with an acidic liquid, such as sour milk, whey, or buttermilk. As a yeast replacement, sourdough is a good alternative. There is a knack to sourdough, but like other skills it can be mastered with practice.

Sourdough is made from flour, water, and airborne yeasts. I find that a little whey helps.

How Much Do We Need?

Calculating how much we need to grow, preserve, and store is another consideration of food self-sufficiency. Initially, my method for doing this was a pretty simple one. I considered how much of a particular food we eat each week, and then figured out how much we'd need on hand until next year's harvest. For example, if we want to eat a quart of green beans each week (two meals for the two of us), then I'll need 52 quarts, whether fresh or preserved. A canner load is 7 quarts, so 6 loads would give me 42 quarts of canned green beans. 7 loads would give me 49. Depending on how long my green beans produce, this will give enough for that quart per week when I can't get fresh. Whenever possible, I like to have extra for company or other occasions.

Another example is fruit for breakfast. Much of this we'll eat fresh: strawberries, peaches, blueberries, figs, and melons in season. These can give us fresh fruit from about May until October frost. This means I'm looking at preserving enough breakfast fruit for 5 or 6 months. If we eat half a pint per day, then I need 3 and ½ pints per week, or about 85 pints for the year. I don't need 85 pints of all peaches, just 85 pints total of all the fruits I have available, either canned or frozen. If I want to use fruits beyond breakfast, say for desserts, then I preserve more. Extra is always handy. Fruit is also desirable for making jams and jellies.

Grains I'm approaching by the trial and error method. The first time we planted field corn, I used 5 pounds of seed. It grew sporadically, but we harvested enough to feed both us and the chickens for almost a year. The second year there was more shade where I planted it, so it didn't produce as well. My plants also showed symptoms of nitrogen deficiency. I chalk these things up to valuable experience and hope that as we improve our soil, we will improve our harvest. The goal is to grow enough corn to feed not only us and the chickens, but pigs too. Each year enough must be saved for seed as well.

In reality, I preserve as much as possible, always hoping to put extra in the pantry regardless of what I consider a year's worth. Some years won't be as plentiful as others, or I may want to give away canned goods as gifts. If for some reason I end up with less of a particular item than I'd hoped for, items in the same category can be substituted. If my green beans do poorly one year, we eat less of those and more of other vegetables. Sometimes our meals may be a little odd by ordinary standards, but we eat well. In the end, we eat what we've got.

My pantry shelves after a summer's work of harvesting, canning, and dehydrating.
A second fridge and small chest freezer store surplus dairy, flour, grains, and seeds.

PRESERVATION & STORAGE

I've already mentioned a number of methods of food preservation: canning, drying, freezing, lacto-fermenting, and root cellaring. There are other methods too, such as brining and smoking both meats and cheeses. One thing living in the southeastern U.S. has taught me, is that not all methods work equally well in every climate. When I was a kid, we would spend summer vacations at a lakeside cottage in Wisconsin. It had several quaint features, including a hand pump in the kitchen instead of a faucet, an outhouse instead of a bathroom, and an ice house. Only the ice house was no longer in use. Today, some homesteaders in the northern US and Canada successfully harvest and utilize stored ice as a preservation method, something we cannot do in the South. Nor can we leave food items outside or in the attic all winter to keep them frozen.

I discovered other regional limitations when I tried root cellaring. Admittedly, I don't have a proper root cellar, but I have tried storing root crops in containers of damp sand in our unheated pantry. While our nighttime winter temperatures usually dip below freezing, our daytime temperatures are too mild, so that those root vegetables were continually sprouting. At the same time I observed that our ground never freezes deeper than surface level, even during the worst of our Southern cold spells. I learned that heavy mulch on the garden beds enables me to leave most of my root crops in the ground all winter long. I can harvest fresh turnips, beets, carrots, parsnips, Jerusalem artichokes, etc., whenever I wish, as long as they're well mulched. The only root crops I have to remove from the ground are potatoes and sweet potatoes. We harvest the potatoes and to keep them from sprouting, I store them in a small, spare refrigerator in the pantry. Eventually, a root cellar might be a good no-energy alternative. Sweet potatoes prefer warmer storage conditions, and do well wrapped in newspaper and stored in a box in the pantry.

Summer presents its challenges too, not only the heat but particularly the humidity. Our high humidity presents problems with dehydrating foods, because items will get moldy before they're well dried. Even with my Excalibur dehydrator I have to take care. I must dry foods almost rock hard before I remove them from the dehydrator. Even stored away in tightly sealed jars, they will soften over time. If dried thoroughly enough, however, they will not become moldy.

Eggs and milk are things we don't usually consider preserving, but on a farm or homestead, these are seasonal items. Chickens stop laying when they moult and lay less during winter's shorter days. Goats must be dried up for two months before they kid. True seasonal living means learning to adapt one's meals to this, although there are preservation techniques for both eggs and milk.

I have learned that eggs freeze very well. I beat them as for scrambled and pour into either ice cube trays or muffin tins. A bit of salt is said to help preserve texture, but I don't always do that. Frozen eggs can be defrosted as needed and honestly, one wouldn't know the difference between frozen or fresh. An option for fresh eggs all winter would be to keep breeds that are known for winter laying.

I find that milk, on the other hand, doesn't freeze well; it becomes grainy when it's defrosted. Plus, it takes up too much freezer space. Still, it is still possible to have year-round milk with goats. One way would be to stagger breeding, so that all does aren't dry at the same time. If some are bred to kid early in the season, and some late, I can have at least one doe in milk at any given time of the year. Another option would be to "milk through", i.e. breed my half of my does every other year, and milking them through their non-breeding year.

This brings up a reality of seasonal living: quantities fluctuate even if I do have a year-round supply. I have to adjust our diet accordingly. With

Freezing eggs. Each muffin cup holds two, well beaten medium size eggs. First, I spray the cups with a vegetable spray so that the frozen eggs are easier to remove.

Making cheese is a way to preserve milk. Rennet is added to make sweet milk curds which are drained from the whey, salted, and pressed into a round cheese.

milk, for example, we consume more dairy products when we have plenty. We can eat lots of kefir, puddings, cream pies, and ice cream, and I use milk instead of water in all my baking, such as bread. Also, during times I have a milk surplus, I make cheese. Any extra beyond all that is fed to the animals: chickens, pigs, dog, and cat.

I recently replaced yogurt in our diet with kefir. The reason for this is because kefir grains multiply, whereas yogurt cultures die out and must be replaced. Kefir enables me to have a self-sustaining supply of cultured milk.

Preserving milk through cheese making is an art form. Like many skills, there is a technical aspect, but there is also a knack to it that is developed with experience. My goal in setting out to learn this skill was not to make the traditional cheeses such as cheddar or Swiss. These require special starter cultures that I would always have to buy. Instead, I've experimented with readily available cultures, such as whey, yogurt, and buttermilk.

What I have been buying is the rennet. Rennet is used to hasten curdling of the milk while it's still sweet, although it will naturally curdle as it sours. Traditional rennet is made from a young calf's (or kid's) stomach, one that has been fed only colostrum. There are directions on the internet for making one's own, though I have no plans at this time to try this. What I do plan to try is experimenting with homemade vegetable rennets from plants I can grow such as yarrow, stinging nettle, fig leaves, lady's bedstraw, ground ivy, thistles, and mallow. All these contain an enzyme which curdles (coagulates) milk.

One question that usually arises when I discuss cheese making is, what do I do with all that whey? Cheese making removes the milk solids and leaves mostly whey. Actually, whey is something I cannot do without. Since reading *Nourishing Traditions*, by Sally Fallon, I have been soaking grains and flours overnight with a bit of whey, to neutralize the phytic acid. This increases digestibility and availability of grain nutrients, but requires a ready supply of whey. I find that we prefer the taste of lacto-fermented foods, such as sauerkraut and sauerruben, if a bit of whey is added. Whey can be used to make a sourdough starter. It helps preserve homemade mayonnaise. It can be substituted for the water or milk in any recipe, including soup. It can be used as a base for a variety of beverages, including lemonade or homemade lacto-fermented soda pop. I've used it to replace part of the water in reconstituted frozen juices. I've already mentioned that I use it as a starter culture in making cheese and fresh whey can also be used to make ricotta cheese. Whey also can be fed to cats, dogs, chickens, and pigs. It retains about a third of the milk's calcium and protein, so it is too nutritious to discard, except on plants as fertilizer.

Common methods of food preservation. Top left: Canning. Top right: Lacto-fermentation. This process naturally preserves foods by souring them with probiotic Lactobacillus bacteria (recipe pg 205). Middle right: Freezing. Some foods, like blueberries, do not need to be blanched. Bottom: Dehydrated summer squash.

Goat cream is slow to rise, so it is skimmed after the milk sits in the refrigerator for several days. I freeze the cream and defrost a jar as needed. Cream for butter works quickest at room temperature and takes 2 to 6 minutes to make.

Hard cheeses are usually waxed to preserve them, and then refrigerated. Cheese can be frozen too, although freezing alters the texture and renders the cheese crumbly. This isn't a problem for grated cheeses, but it does take up freezer space. Instead I wax and store my hard cheeses in my pantry refrigerator. I do freeze my mozzarella. I grate it first and for my purposes (pizza mostly), it doesn't matter if it's crumbly.

There are two milk products I do freeze: colostrum and cream. Colostrum is necessary for newborn kids, so I keep it just in case. Also I freeze cream. Contrary to what many believe, goats' milk is not naturally homogenized and the cream can indeed be collected. The key is to allow it to sit for several days before skimming. I collect it by skimming with a spoon. I put it in pint mason jars and store them in the freezer. I defrost a jar as needed to make butter or whipped cream.

Butter can be preserved freezing or clarifying (known as ghee). I've also seen a two piece French style butter keeper in my Lehman's catalog. A small, butter packed bowl is placed upside-down in an accompanying crock, which is filled with cold water. This creates an air tight seal to preserve the butter, while keeping it soft enough to spread.

Working Toward No-Energy
Food Preservation & Storage

Besides food self-sufficiency, another of our goals is energy self-sufficiency. This is a long term goal, so I analyze food preservation in the light of that. Our warm climate and frequent humid days present several challenges to keeping and preserving food. On the other hand, our climate enables us to eat seasonally from the garden almost all year long. The menu is less varied, but we have the potential to feed ourselves with minimal food preservation.

Of the various food preservation techniques, freezing and refrigeration, of course, require electricity. Although propane refrigerators are available, we would not consider this an option. I confess I was initially a bit hesitant to buy a chest freezer for food preservation, because of our long term goal of energy self-sufficiency. I don't deny that it has been extremely useful, especially for preserving meats and things like eggs, cream, strawberries, and blueberries. Also for freezing tomatoes as a method of easily peeling them (see page 173). Still, our area is prone to severe ice storms in winter which can knock out electricity for days at a time. That causes me to be aware of what, and how much I store in my freezer. Some of the best uses for my freezer have been to store grains to protect them from pantry moths, and to store water. Freezing water not only keeps it for emergencies, but will also help keep the freezer cold in case we do lose electricity. If we were without power for too long, the contents of my freezer, such as meat, could be canned. I am, in fact, beginning to can more meats, with a future view toward going off-grid.

Canning ordinarily requires electricity too, although it can be done over wood heat. With reusable canning lids, it can be an extremely self-sustaining way of preserving food. (For more information on those, see "Tattler Reusable Canning Lids" listed in Appendix A.)

Solar dehydrators work well in dry climates, but because of our humidity I have not yet been successful with that. I currently use an Excalibur electric food dehydrator, and have also discovered that my wood cookstove is excellent for dehydrating foods. My method is simple, I spread the chopped food out on cookie sheets, set these in the open-doored oven, and keep a moderate fire going. This dries food beautifully, but it's use for that purpose is limited because I do not use the wood cookstove during summer. Plans for a stovetop food dehydrator for wood cookstoves can be found in Jane Cooper's *Woodstove Cookery*. This may be something

If one doesn't have a root cellar, turnips can kept in damp sand inside a cooler. Stored in an unheated room, they will keep fresh during cold winter months.

I'll have to consider in the future, especially if we ever get a second wood cookstove for an outdoor kitchen. In fact, an outdoor kitchen for outdoor summer cooking is on our longterm "to do" list. Hopefully, it will incorporate not only a charcoal/wood grill, but also an oven for baking and a smoker.

Besides an outdoor kitchen I'd like to have a root cellar someday. I previously mentioned that I was unsuccessful with root cellaring techniques in our unheated pantry because I couldn't keep the room temperature consistently cool enough to prevent sprouting. Leaving turnips, beets, parsnips, Jerusalem artichokes, and carrots heavily mulched in the garden is no-energy, but using the refrigerator to store potatoes is not. Because it uses the earth's temperature, a root cellar may be the best no-energy way for me to store not only potatoes, but pumpkins, sweet potatoes, winter squashes, sauerkraut, and other lacto-fermented foods.

Lacto-fermenting is a traditional way of preserving foods, especially vegetables. It does not require refrigeration, although the foods will continue to sour the longer they sit. Some people can their sauerkraut when it reaches the flavor they prefer. Canning destroys the living bacteria and enzymes, but will prevent further souring.

Other methods I have yet to try include brining and smoking meats. I'd love to learn how to make those gourmet Italian meats, preserved by salting and either smoking or air-drying (doubtful in our humidity). Even more non-electric preservation techniques include preserving in oil, vinegar, salt, sugar, and alcohol. Directions for these can be found in the book, *Preserving Food Without Freezing or Canning* (see Appendix A.)

Perpetuating The Food Supply

The last aspect of a self-sustaining food supply is to keep it coming. In the garden, this primarily means seed saving. I mentioned it previously, but it's worth mentioning again because if one's goal is to be food self-sufficient, saving seed is no less important than the food itself.

The most important rule about seed saving is to save seed only from open-pollinated varieties of plants. The seeds from these will produce plants "true to type," i.e. they will produce plants just like their parents. Heirloom types are always open-pollinated, as are some of the more modern varieties.

Hybrid seeds, on the other hand, are bred from specifically chosen parent plants to produce specifically selected traits: disease resistance, earlier production, higher yield, better shipping qualities or marketing characteristics, etc. The seeds from hybrid plants are often sterile, and so will not sprout. Or, they may produce a "throwback" to one or the other parent, which may not have the qualities a home gardener is looking for.

Easiest to save are seeds that can dry on the plant, such as beans. As long as they are gathered before the pods shatter and scatter the seed, they are easy to save. For beans, I allow the pods to dry, pick them, shell the seed, and store in air-tight containers in the refrigerator.

More challenging to gather and save, are seeds from fleshy vegetables such as tomatoes, cucumbers, and squashes. It's best to allow these to become overripe before scooping out the seed into a container. About a quarter cup of water is added, and the pulp allowed to ferment until it no longer clings to the seeds. The seeds are then drained, rinsed, and dried.

Most seeds can remain viable for several years if properly stored. Some, such as corn, onions, and parsnips have a short "shelf life" and can be kept for only a year or two at best. Beans and peas remain viable for about three years. Most other seeds remain viable longer than that, up to five years. The key here is that the seeds are dried properly and kept in an airtight container away from heat and humidity.

Many seeds are simple to save, like these black turtle beans.

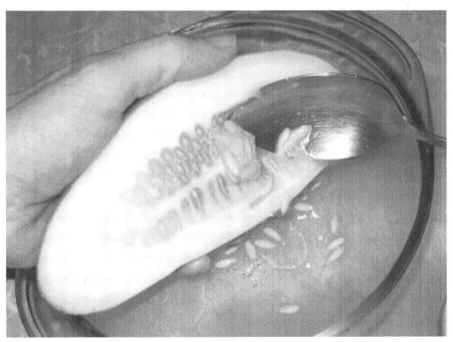

Cucumber seeds with pulp being scooped into a bowl. Water is added and the mixture stirred daily to prevent mold from forming. In few days, the seeds separate from the pulp. Then they are drained, rinsed, dried, and stored away.

A Welsummer hen with Buff Orpington and Barred Holland chicks. Roosters are not necessary for hens to lay eggs, but they are necessary for the eggs to hatch.

My particular challenge with seed saving has been cross-pollination. There are techniques to deal with this, including staggering planting times so that different varieties of the same vegetable aren't pollinating at the same time. Also flowers can be covered and hand pollinated. I tend to migrate toward the simplest methods. I don't have to save all seeds every year, so I consider things like rotating cross-pollinators annually.

Lastly, having self-sustaining animal products such as eggs and milk means learning how to breed animals. This includes learning how to keep and manage (in our case) roosters and bucks. Alternatives to keeping a buck would be to take our does elsewhere to be bred. Since we have the space and can feed them, we opt to keep bucks ourselves. While a rooster is not necessary for chickens to lay eggs, he is necessary for them to lay fertile eggs, and hence raise one's own chickens.

Conclusion

Before I conclude this chapter, there is one "mistake" I'd like to mention. At least I think it's a mistake. It's one that homesteaders often make when they begin to pursue the goal of working toward food self-sufficiency. It is that people tend to compare the cost of what they produce for themselves with price tags at the grocery store. For some reason, we all end up doing this at one point or another, usually about the time we realize how much work it will take to have a self-sustaining food supply. More times than not, the conclusion is that growing our own food is far more expensive than shopping at the grocery store.

On a cursory level, this often appears to be true, especially in the beginning, when we are spending so much time and money getting started. Initially, we must invest in tools, seeds, plants, preservation equipment, compost production, garden set-up, mulch, etc. Soil preparation in the beginning is hard work, as is learning what grows well in our region. It takes time to develop the sense of seasons and the routine of the whole thing. It takes time and practice to learn the various food preservation and seed saving techniques. Eventually all these things are no longer a factor. The initial expenses are mostly one-time rather than ongoing. As we develop the knowledge, skills, and a routine, our time is more efficiently spent as well.

Even so, the comparison of grocery store food with homegrown is not an accurate one. What is on grocery store shelves is commercially produced. Artificial ingredients and preservatives aside, the quality of food suffers because the ways and means of industrialized agriculture focus on quantity and profit, not quality and nutrition, nor on the well-being of their soil and their animals. Are my eggs, produced by free-ranged chickens who eat bugs, worms, seeds, grains, fruits and vegetables, equal in quality and value to factory eggs, produced by chickens who are fed formulated pellets, breathe ammonia contaminated air because of overcrowding, and live 24 hours a day under the glare of artificial lighting? Or can I really compare my pure raw goat milk to ultra-pasteurized, rBGH (recombinant, i.e. genetically modified, bovine growth hormone) grocery store milk? Then there are the added values of manure for the compost, increases in flock and herd, meat and/or sales from culling, plus the peace of mind from knowing what I'm eating, what's in my food, what my animals have been fed, and that they've been well cared for. Shouldn't these be factored into the value of producing one's own food?

That this is a question at all is a reflection of our social conditioning. At one time it was considered patriotic to grow one's own garden, now it is not. Now, society has taught us to rate everything on a scale of monetary value. The question, is it worth it to grow my own food, ought to be based on how well it helps us meet our goals, rather than whether or not we're saving money by doing it. And that goes back to our mindset regarding why we want to be food self-sufficient in the first place. Am I seeking to

Foods we can produce ourselves: eggs, tomatoes, grain for flour, cream for butter, and pumpkin for pumpkin muffins, all make for rewarding homestead eating.

raise my own food to gain a financial benefit or a return on an investment? Or because I want to eat real food, to know where it comes from? Maybe I'm motivated by environmental concerns or simply for the love of doing it. Perhaps I do it because of concerns for the way our world food supply is being managed, and for the sense of purpose, security, and freedom, food self-sufficiency offers.

In terms of evaluating the worth of our food, I honestly think money is a poor standard of value. If I look at my garden harvest and consider only what it's worth in terms of money, I must realize that its value is unstable and changes as conditions fluctuate. Yet, I always need to eat. That doesn't change. It doesn't change if produce is worth 25 cents a pound, or if it's worth $5 a pound. I still need to eat.

For the homesteader, the questions about raising one's own food should be personal and ethical, not financial and economical. The questions we need to ask ourselves are: How do I want to nourish my body, my family? What kind of food do I want to eat? How do I want it grown? How do I want it preserved? Do I want to contribute to the environmental problems created by modern agribusiness practices, or help heal them? What are my self-sufficiency goals and how does raising my own food help meet them? Whether or not the cost of raising one's own food is worth it will depend upon one's answers.

For Dan and me, our long-term goal is to decrease our need for money and our dependence on the consumer system. Our biggest concerns are for the quality of food being sold today, especially the artificial methods and ingredients being used, and the unnatural means by which our food sources are being developed and processed. We see a direct correlation between that and health, both human and environmental. Raising our own food is a top priority and for us, that means raising all or most of our own animal feed as well. How much of that we can grow will ultimately determine the number of animals we can keep; we must strive for a balance. We also understand that it will take time to accomplish this goal. It will be a step by step process, but will enable our homestead to be more self-sustaining in the long run.

In the end, there are no one-size-fits-all solutions to the challenges of achieving food self-sufficiency. It not only depends upon personal food preferences and requirements, but on geographical location as well. My advice to anyone wishing to start, is to start with whatever is at hand. It is better to grow one potted tomato plant on the patio than none at all. It is better to have a small suburban garden than none at all. It is better to keep a few potted herbs under a grow light than none at all. It is better to do something rather than nothing. By starting one step at a time, you may be amazed at where the journey can take you.

NOTES

[1] Gene Logsdon, *Small-Scale Grain Raising* (White River Junction, VT: Chelsea Green Publishing, 2009) 79

[2] Irma S. Rombauer, and Marion Rombauer Becker, *Joy Of Cooking* (Indianapolis: Bobbs-Merrill Co. Inc. 1980) 555

CHAPTER 7

FOOD SELF-SUFFICIENCY: FEEDING OUR ANIMALS

Our first kid born on the homestead was a buckling. Happily, labor and delivery went smoothly. His daddy's name was Petey, so we named him RePete.

Animals are an important part of our homestead. They provide eggs, milk, meat, manure, young for increase or to trade or sell, endless hours of entertainment, and give us a sense of purpose and joy. It has been important to consider how they fit into our overall goal of self-sufficiency. We decided, in the beginning, that each animal must contribute to our needs, and that we, in turn, must not keep more than our land can properly provide for. The last thing we want is to end up with an impressive, but expensive, petting zoo.

Feeding our animals from the land is a long-term goal. Although we felt we had enough land for grazing a small herd of goats, it would take

Hay was the first thing we harvested for our goats. Dan purchased a scythe and used it to cut our weedy, one acre hay field. We hauled it off in the wheelbarrow.

time to fence it all in. When the grass in our unfenced field grew tall, we decided to use it for hay. Dan bought a scythe and cut about an acre by hand. We let it dry on the ground, raked it, hauled it with the wheelbarrow, and made a huge haystack near the goat shed. It was satisfying work.

Chicken and goat feed had to be purchased, however, and it didn't take long to discover that any grocery budget savings I realized from producing our own vegetables, fruits, eggs, milk, cheese, butter, kefir, and meat was lost on animal feed. While I wasn't spending more because of our critters, neither was I spending less. In addition, almost all animal feeds (including pet foods) are based on the largest commercially produced, often genetically modified crops, particularly corn and soy. We began to discuss what it would take to grow their feed ourselves.

I admit the whole prospect seemed overwhelming at first. We had cleared acreage but were uncertain of how many animals it could support. If we grew grain and hay we would need more fencing to keep the animals out until we could harvest. But what would we grow? What would best meet our animals' needs? What would grow well in our area? How much land would it take? How much would it produce? How much would we need for a year's worth? What equipment would we need? How would we harvest it? How would we process it? Where would we store it?

I am a firm believer that experience is the best teacher so we decided to simply make a start. I didn't know what would grow well in our part of the country so I planted small plots in the garden to learn: corn, wheat, barley, oats, amaranth, cowpeas, and black oil sunflowers. The following spring we chose an area and fenced it off for growing field crops.

We cleared the sapling pine trees but still needed to turn the heavy, weedy soil in order to plant the seeds. The problem was that we don't have the equipment to plow the ground. Dan looked at used tractors, but didn't want to pay several thousand dollars for a machine that needed major repairs to get it running. We looked into renting, but no one rented tractors with plow attachments. We could rent one with a bush hog but not with a plow. Thankfully, our neighbor had a tractor with a tiller attachment and kindly agreed to do this for us. We hand planted half of our new grain field in field corn, the other half in black oil sunflowers.

The sunflowers did not do well because of competition with the weeds: morning glories, blackberry vines, saw briars, kudzu, and others.

Cattle panel hay feeder; cheap and easy to make but wastes a lot of hay.

They engulfed everything. The corn gave us a respectable harvest, but only because it grew taller than the weeds and I could find it. Getting to it was the other problem, because the weeds were so thick.

We followed the corn with winter wheat. We had several problems with that, most significantly nitrogen deficiency. This wasn't a surprise. We already knew the soil was poor and that it would take time to get it built up in each of our fields. The corn, being a heavy feeder of nitrogen, had probably used the little that was there. I had manure, fish emulsion, and blood meal on hand, but not enough to improve the situation. This reinforced how badly we needed a plan for soil improvement. We accepted the problems as learning experiences, knowing we were acquiring the knowledge to make things better.

The following spring we planted corn again, but in a previously unplanted part of the field. This time I planted the rows far enough apart so that I could keep the weeds cut back with my lawn mower. By this time, I had done quite a bit of research on animal nutrition and was looking for a good source of protein for both chickens and goats. I planted a section with a small type of cowpea, Ozark Razorback, for that reason.

We learned a lot from doing this. We were beginning to get an idea of what we could grow and what it would take. Harvesting hadn't been too terribly difficult but processing and storing were things for which we were not well prepared. We learned that some things don't need to be processed. Cowpeas could be fed pods and all to the goats, and the chickens knew exactly what to do with whole wheat heads. We knew we still had a lot to learn, but at least we had a start.

Doing The Research

Initially I had two books on livestock, *Raising Dairy Goats the Modern Way* by Jerry Belanger, and *Raising Poultry The Modern Way* by Leonard S. Mercia. These were the resources I referred to for answers to my questions. The more I read, however, the more discouraged I became. The subject of animal feed was apparently quite complex. I didn't even have a local source for some of the ingredients, like fish meal for chicken feed. Nor would I be able to process things like soybeans on a large scale. And where could I obtain the bulk vitamins and minerals that needed to be added? And at what cost?

It finally occurred to me that, as homesteaders, we had different goals than the authors of these books. These were geared toward making a

Two good reasons to get goats: kudzu (left) and poison ivy (below).

Kudzu, Pueraria lobata, "the vine that ate the South." Kudzu was introduced to the United States in 1876 at the Centennial Exposition in Philadelphia. By the 1930s the U.S. government was paying farmers $8 an acre to plant it for erosion control. In 1997 Congress placed kudzu on the Federal Noxious Weed list.[1] Currently estimated to cover 7 million acres in the southeastern U.S, goats have been found to be an effective means of control.

One of our fields was covered with poison ivy when we bought the place. It carpeted the ground and grew up the trees. We consumed the milk from our poison ivy eating goats that summer, and discovered something interesting; we both developed an immunity to poison ivy. Dan, especially, who is extremely sensitive to it, had only mild cases, and I had none. While science has yet to confirm this, I have heard from others who have experienced the same thing.

business of it, toward production and profit, rather than keeping a few animals for what they can provide for one family. The production approach assumes a large number of animals in more confined, controlled conditions. Scientifically formulated feed mixes must accommodate for this, providing every nutrient except water in one pellet. Dan and I planned to allow our animals to free range and forage. We wanted to supplement their diet rather than make complete feed mixes ourselves.

On the other hand, I realized it would be a mistake to oversimplify the whole thing and think, well, back in the day they didn't feed them anything other than what they could grow. Back in the day, soils hadn't eroded as much and soil nutrients hadn't been used up and leached out. Still, I had the ability to build the soil, which would enable me to grow nutritious foods for our livestock as well as ourselves.

I turned to the internet to do my research and began to glean helpful information on home mixed feeds for goats and chickens. By reading forums and blogs, I discovered people with similar interests who were discussing this very topic. Some had self-sufficiency goals like Dan and I, others were discussing it because they were not convinced that packaged feeds were the best thing for their animals. Even then, there appeared to be many ideas, preferences, even controversy over what to feed various species. While I learned a great deal from the online forums and other bloggers, I walked away with more questions.

One topic of discussion that interested me was the differences between modern commercial breeds of animals and the traditional breeds, also referred to as heritage breeds. I had assumed that the interest in keeping heritage breeds was for novelty and conservation. While this is true, I learned there is more to it.

The modern breeds of livestock have been developed for one purpose - production. They need to be able to efficiently convert feed to the end product: milk, eggs, and meat. They must be able to tolerate confinement and grow quickly to a target weight. This minimizes the expense of feed and housing and increases profit. Scientifically formulated feeds have been developed with this goal in mind. Consider poultry where some commercial meat breeds become so heavy that they can barely walk. They do, however, quickly produce plump, meaty legs and breasts, and dress out beautifully for styrofoam packages in the grocery store.

Heritage breeds, on the other hand, will not produce to grocery store standards. The advantage for homesteaders is that their natural instincts have not been bred out of them. Traditional breeds of poultry still know how to forage, mate, and mother. Most of these are considered dual

Some folks separate the kids and bottle feed them. We let the kids stay with their mothers. We have to share the milk, but it saves work and is healthier for the goats.

purpose, and can provide both eggs and meat. The trade-off is that they do not produce as many eggs as the commercial layers, nor are they as meaty as the broiler breeds. Those of us used to lots of tender white breast meat when we sit down to a roast chicken dinner are in for a disappointment the first time we roast up a Delaware or Buff Orpington.

This applies to other species as well. Modern dairy goats are bred for milk production. Nubian does, for example, can put every ounce of what they consume into making milk, until they are nothing but skin and bones. I had a doe like this. She looked like a walking skeleton after she kidded, no matter how much I fed her. I thought I was doing something wrong because our Pygmy buck kept his belly big and bulging on pasture and hay alone. As I scoured the goat forums for answers, I learned I wasn't the only one with this problem; others sometimes had trouble keeping weight on their milking does too. Goats like this are not considered "easy keepers." However, they are doing what they were bred to do, i.e. plentifully produce rich, creamy milk.

As I studied feeding livestock, I learned that while their nutritional needs are similar to humans, i.e. they need protein, carbohydrates, fats, vitamins, and minerals, they do not necessarily digest food like we do. Chickens, for example, can readily eat grains but have no teeth. Instead they have a gizzard which contains the grit they consume. The grit is not digestible but acts to grind the grain like teeth. Chickens also have a crop, where grains are predigested with amylase, an enzyme that breaks down the indigestible coating on grains and seeds.

Goats, on the other hand, are ruminants. Like cows and sheep, they have four stomachs called rumen. This kind of digestive system is best suited for grass, hay, and forage. Grains, being slower to digest, begin to ferment in the rumen and lower its pH, making it more acidic. This can develop into a condition called acidosis, which can be fatal to goats. This is why slow changes are advised when changing feeds; it allows time for the intestinal flora to adjust. Also, it's why many goat owners offer baking soda free choice on the side, to neutralize an acidic gut. Acidosis can be avoided by minimizing the amount of grain, or by feeding no grain at all.

One important consideration in feed is protein. Milk, eggs, and meat are largely protein, and I found lots of information and discussion about this. I was used to human nutrition, however, and thought in terms of complete proteins and essential amino acids. Animal scientists, on the other hand, speak of crude protein (CP) and digestible protein. Crude protein is the nitrogen content of a feed. Digestible protein is what the animal can utilize.

Milking does are said to need a feed ration of 16% crude protein in addition to hay. Laying hens are said to need 16 to 18%. How they came up with those figures, I don't know. Because these percentages are higher than what most grains, hay, and forage contain, it puzzled me as to how to achieve a consistent 16% protein content in a natural diet.

This is especially true for goats, which are herbivores. Chickens, being omnivorous, and will naturally get quite a bit of protein from eating bugs, worms, and grubs if allowed to free range.

In commercial feeds, the protein source is usually soy. Soy appears to be controversial for several reasons. One is that most of the soy grown in the United States is genetically modified. While not everyone is convinced that genetically modified foods are a problem, many people want to avoid them. Even if organic soybeans can be grown or obtained, soy must either be processed to be digestible, or offered in limited quantities. In addition, soy is high in phytohormones which can cause thyroid and other hormone related problems in humans as well as animals. For all these reasons, I decided against using soy. At 35 to 45% crude protein, however, it is hard to match in a feed mix.

Mama hens will drop bits of feed to the ground for their chicks.

Once common source of protein for goats is alfalfa hay. Often fed as pellets, it supplies 16% protein and is an excellent source of calcium too. Unfortunately, it doesn't grow well in my part of the country, so I had to look for alternatives. Although not commonly used, one such alternative would seem to be comfrey. At 22 to 33% protein, it can be fed fresh (the goats love it) or dried like hay. Plus it provides calcium. Other protein possibilities we could potentially grow include black oil sunflower seeds (BOSS) at 17% crude protein, field peas at 23%, and flax seed at 35% CP.

The question this raised was how to mix what I grew so as to get a target protein content. If one year I harvested 100 pounds of wheat (13% CP), 50 pounds of grain sorghum (10% CP), 90 pounds of cowpeas (23% CP), and 45 pounds of black oil sunflower seeds (16% CP), how would I know what amounts to mix to get say, 16%?

An internet acquaintance emailed about this time and sent some website links for something called the Pearson Square. This is a tool that can be used to calculate a ratio of any two components for a particular mix. It was originally developed to standardize the fat and protein contents in commercially produced milk, but has since been used for wine making,

Six week old Buff Orpington chicks drinking whey from cheese making. Whey provides much needed protein and calcium for both chicks and laying hens.

juice mixing, cheese making, baking, and of course, feed formulation. I've included a step-by-step explanation with examples in Appendix B.

Protein for the chickens is easier to manage. If allowed to free range, they'll hunt out larvae and insects. The bonus here is that they help keep the bug population under control. Also, chickens love raw goat milk, whey, meat scraps, bits of dried or moldy cheese, and grubs from the garden. Protein for chickens is one reason we put in a compost worm bed.

Minerals are my second concern. The milk and whey I feed to the chickens also provides them with much needed calcium for egg shell production. So do those egg shells themselves. Dried and finely crushed, the chickens love them and do not recognize them as eggs (and become egg eaters). Between these two things, our hens' egg shells are strong and hard without supplementing their diet with oyster shells (something I can't produce for myself).

Dairy goats also need calcium, as well as a number of other key minerals. These and vitamins are added to commercial feed pellets, but if I mix my own feeds from whole grains, seeds, and legumes, this is something else I need to address. Initially I bought a generic mineral salt block, but soon learned that experienced goat owners prefer a free choice loose goat mineral because goats get more of what they need this way. Also I learned that various mineral deficiencies are regional, and sometimes have to be addressed in spite of the additives in the formulated feeds and mineral mixes. Copper and selenium are the two most common examples, and I learned this is a problem in our area too.

The book that helped me the most on the subject of minerals was (and still is) Pat Coleby's *Natural Goat Care*. She particularly discusses the importance of minerals in the goat diet, their role in health, and how they work in conjunction with other nutrients. Also I was interested that she feeds her goats less protein than American producers. She writes that many of the modern health problems goats have are related to high protein and mineral deficiencies. What really caught my attention was the idea of remineralizing the soil to improve the nutritional quality of hay and forage. In her book, Pat quotes agronomist Neal Kinsey often. This set me to looking for more information and I discovered his book, *Hands-On Agronomy*, by the same publisher, Acres U.S.A., (www.acresusa.com).

Theoretically, animals should get all their vitamins and minerals from their diet. Usually they don't, because if the grains and grasses are grown on mineral deficient soils, these will be deficient as well. It follows, then, that their manure will also be deficient, so that as compost, it will still not add missing nutrients to the soil. This is a cycle that requires intervention if we want our land and our animals to be healthy. Remineralizing the soil made sense to me. How much better for our animals to get their minerals directly from what they eat, rather than from a formulated supplement. I began to research further and we worked on a plan to improve soil quality in each field, one at a time.

PUTTING IT ALL TOGETHER

As I have mentioned, our longterm goal is to feed our livestock entirely from our own land. We want their primary source of food to be from foraging. This can be from either field or woods, of which we have both. For goats, pasture areas will need to include a variety of grasses, legumes, and herbs. During production periods or when weather conditions warrant, we will supplement their diets with hay, grain, legumes, seeds, nuts, and garden produce. Because our winters are relatively mild, cool weather grasses, legumes, and vegetables can still grow. Theoretically, at least, we should be able to offer natural forage all year long.

Scraping the poison ivy field, also pictured on page 87. To prepare our first field for remineralization and planting, we rented a skid loader to scrape off the vines and seedling trees. We lost very little top soil because there wasn't much there.

Working toward this goal has not been without its challenges. Our first field crops gave us badly needed practical experience, and my research gave me much needed information about proper nutrition for goats. But it also raised questions as to whether or not we will be able to provide everything our animals need. Nutrition can be a very complex subject and while I do want our animals to be properly fed, I do not want to be spending endless hours trying to analyze nutrient content, calculate feed ratios, and balance feed rations.

We know our soil is poor so soil improvement is foundational. If I feed the soil, then I feed the plants, which will feed our animals, and us. After reading Neal Kinsey's *Hands-On Agronomy* we decided to test the soil in our pastures, one at a time, utilizing the services of a professional soil testing company. This is more expensive than having it tested through our state cooperative extension service, but the results are more extensive and include the micronutrients about which we are concerned. We chose Kinsey Agricultural Services, not only because I liked his book, but because we could get recommendations for organic mineral amendments if we wanted, rather than chemical fertilizers.

It was trying to track down those amendments that became a challenge. Locally I could find limestone by the ton. I could find natural phosphorous as bone meal and nitrogen as blood meal, but only in expensive three pounds packages. I needed 500 pounds of phosphates and 425 pounds of nitrogen for the half acre field we were working on. To go the three pound package route would have cost me more than $2000 for those two alone. Also I needed magnesium, boron, manganese, and cobalt. I found them in specialized organic mixes, azalea or rose food for example, but locally I could not find them as individual soil amendments, except boron, which I purchased as borax on the laundry aisle at the grocery store.

It took about six months to find sources for everything we needed. My local feed store could order some, the rest I would need to mail order. Shipping was expensive but we viewed this project as an investment in our land so we bit the bullet. The hardest thing to find was cobalt sulfate. Goats need cobalt to synthesize vitamin B12, but no nursery company seemed to carry it. I was finally able to order it from a ceramics supply house because it is used in blue glazes for pottery.

We chose our poorest field for that first remineralization project. Like the grain field it was badly overgrown with blackberry brambles, but also it contained a sea of poison ivy. Hundreds of sapling pecans, sweet gums, and cedar trees were trying to grow there as well. The lesson learned from the corn field was that simply tilling wouldn't be enough to get rid of all this. It seemed drastic but we finally decided to rent a skid loader to scrape away the trees and vines. Then we mixed the minerals in a wheelbarrow, broadcast them over the field by hand, and once again, our neighbor tilled them in for us. I planted it with a mix of grasses, legumes, root vegetables, and herbs. After the next rain we were rewarded with the beautiful fresh green growth of a newly planted pasture. Five months later, we were able to turn the goats in for their first taste.

Establishing our first pasture and growing field crops felt like major accomplishments, but the field crops presented another new challenge - processing. We knew it had to be done but did not envision what it would take to process hundreds of pounds worth. Some things we have managed with the proper tools, things like sunflower seeds. Black oil sunflower seeds (BOSS) are soft shelled and can be fed whole (i.e. unhulled) to goats. That means I only have to remove the seeds from the heads, not shell them. I do this by rubbing the heads over hardware cloth framed in a box (page 97).

Corn is easy to hand harvest and husk, and fairly easy to shell. Two dried ears can be rubbed together, or a sheller can be used. We purchased a hand crank sheller (pictured page 98) that works very well.

To prevent bloat, introduction to the new pasture was slow, increasing grazing about 15 minutes per day. This gave the goats' intestinal microbes time to adjust.

The cowpeas, like any dried bean or pea, are time-consuming to shell by hand. Electric shellers are available for several hundred dollars, but I found a reasonably priced hand-crank sheller that works quite well (page 98). When a comment on my blog suggested the goats might eat the peas in the shell, I offered some and was pleased to find that this is true. It means less work on my part and adds bulk and roughage to their winter diets.

Wheat has been the most difficult to process. We've tried a number of hand threshing methods. All involve various means of pounding the wheat heads to loosen the grains and then winnowing with a box fan to remove the chaff. While this is feasilble for small amounts, it isn't for the hundreds of pounds we need for goat feed. Fortunately, it doesn't need to be threshed for chickens.

Besides field crops and pasture, I have been learning how to garden and forage for our animals. Produce can be fed fresh, stored, or dried to supplement their diet, especially during winter months. Vegetables, fruits, and herbs contain vitamins and minerals, which makes them key for a self-sufficient livestock feeding program. Other things, such as autumn acorns, provide much needed carbohydrates and fats for the goats' winter diet.

Another thing we learned was to turn our animals into the grain field after we harvested. The remnants of our field crops make excellent forage for both chickens and goats. They feast not only on the leftover stalks, dropped seeds, and dried leaves, but especially on the weeds. We do not use synthetic herbicides and we do not have a cultivator, so our corn, sunflowers, wheat, and cowpeas are always loaded with weeds.

That simple act was actually quite a revelation in another area of our lives. We had a certain mindset about how the place is supposed to look. Weeds as tall as the corn and beans do not contribute to our sense of a picturesque, well-managed looking homestead. Earlier in the summer, I had unsuccessfully battled those weeds in an attempt to make the corn look like we knew what we were doing. Seeing our goats thrive on what what we thought was an eyesore made me realize that my idea of manageability carries with it a certain mindset about the way things ought to be. My concept of well-managed includes looking like we've got things under control. A near half acre full of weeds looks out of control. That isn't part of the definition.

Hardware cloth stapled to a wood frame makes it easy to separate sunflower seeds from the heads. Simply rub the heads on the mesh and catch them in a container below, in this case, my wheelbarrow.

Above: Hand crank pea sheller shelling dried Ozark Razorback cowpeas. Our goats eat pods and all, but for us and the chickens they need to be shelled first. This variety is a small, heirloom Southern Pea, akin to well-known black-eyed peas.

Left: Hand crank corn sheller. This recently manufactured version of a classic old farm tool is cleverly designed. The spikes on the plate rotate the ear of corn as they pop off the kernels and eject the cob out the side. For the homesteader, this tool makes swift work of the otherwise tedious job of hand shelling dried corn.

In truth, goats prefer weeds, shrubs, bark, and leaves; all the things that don't belong in a well-managed pasture or grain field. These deep rooted plants pull minerals from deep within the soil, making them healthier for goats than short rooted grasses. This is why our goats deem the pretty, pure grass, boughten hay merely okay, but fight over the weedy hay we harvest from our own fields. Because of that, I am learning not to see my weedy crops as eyesores, but as rich forage for my animals.

How far along are we in achieving our goal to feed our animals from our land? I'd say we've made some progress but still have a way to go. For the chickens I am able to replace store bought chicken scratch with homegrown for at least part of the year. I offer them shelled field corn and unthreshed whole wheat heads, and toss a head of amaranth into the chicken yard to round out the routine. They also get a handful or two of black oil sunflower seeds or shelled cowpeas, and fresh greens when available. Between these things, kitchen scraps, grubs and worms I collect from the garden, plus their free ranging, I find I need to buy less packaged chicken feed, which is offered free choice in their feeder.

We've been cutting our own hay from our weedy pastures since the first summer we had goats. To this I now add dried kudzu, grasses and weeds I cut down along the fence with my hand-held sickle. Also things we can grow in small areas, such as buckwheat or vetch.

I still purchase most of the goats' daily feed ration, but I am mixing it myself rather than buying a complete pelleted formulation. I want to control what goes into their feed, as well as assure myself that my goats were getting whole grain rather than "plant protein products", "plant roughage products", and other plant waste filler glued together with molasses. I choose not to include the most common genetically engineered ingredients (corn and soy). My grain mix is made from wheat, oats, and barley when I can get it. This mix is topped off with black oil sunflower seeds, a few pods of cowpeas, and a huge scoop of non-GMO alfalfa pellets. These are all things we can grow or gather ourselves, except alfalfa, which does not do well in this part of the country. However, I am able to replace some of the alfalfa pellets with comfrey, which is also rich in protein and calcium. My plan is to eventually grow and harvest enough comfrey to replace purchased alfalfa pellets altogether.

This ration is fed to pregnant and milking does, bucks during mating season, and all goats during winter when the forage is poorer. I'm hoping that as the quality of our pasture and forage is improved, plus made available all year long, I will need to offer less feed during winter to keep my goats in top condition.

Hay can be more than grass and legumes. Top left: Russian Comfrey Bocking #4, a sterile, non-spreading hybrid. Top right: Wheelbarrow of hand-sickle cut grass and weeds from along a fence line. Bottom: A patch of buckwheat in flower.

Anything goats eat fresh can be dried for hay. Comfrey can be fed fresh or dried as can kudzu, and grasses and weeds growing along fences. Small plots around fruit trees can be planted with things like buckwheat, which acts as a ground cover, improves the soil, can be dried for hay, and provides edible seeds called groats.

Gardening and foraging for my goats is an area in which I have made good progress. I plant as much in my garden as I can, with the idea that the extra will be fed to our animals, some fresh, and some dried. They also get scraps from the kitchen and from food preservation. I feed them greens such as collards, kale, turnip, beet, Swiss chard, cabbage, broccoli, and dandelion. They can eat all of the root crops expect potatoes: carrots, beets, turnips, mangels, parsnips, sugar beets, sweet potatoes, radishes, and Jerusalem artichokes. While sweet potatoes have to be stored, I can harvest the other root crops all winter long if the beds are well mulched. Many greens will grow during winter if the weather is mild or we can use row covers or a hoop house.

Squashes include both summer and winter varieties as well as pumpkins. Melons too, the goats can eat the rind, seeds, and pulp of all of these, the chickens go for the seeds and pulp. Other things include corn leaves (also broom corn and sorghum varieties) sweet potato vines (which I have discovered boost milk production), berries, and peelings from things like cucumber and tomatoes. Of tomatoes, I only feed the fruits. The leaves and vines are not permitted because tomatoes are members of the nightshade family, which are poisonous to goats.

While there is nominal protein in produce, it is a valuable source of roughage, carbohydrates, vitamins, and minerals. The importance of roughage often seems to be lost in the debates over grains, proteins, and minerals, or maybe it's just taken for granted. Labeled "crude fiber" on the feed bag labels, it is necessary for keeping goats' digestive systems healthy.

I forage for my goats as well. While I need to be aware that certain plants can poison goats (rhododendron or azalea, for example), they get all the yard trimmings. Also I discovered they love acorns. A good source of carbohydrates and fats, the goats will forage for these themselves, but also I'll sweep up panfuls for them from the yard. In addition, surplus harvest of berries, rose hips, herbs, even greens can be dehydrated and fed to the chickens or added to a goat's ration as a top dressing for extra vitamins and minerals, especially in winter. (See Appendix C for a listing of these). Other things fall into this category, like dried oak and pecan leaves, also corn tops and leaves, taking care not feed them anything moldy.

Of course, what they *can* eat and what they will eat aren't necessarily the same. An item at which goats turn up their noses during summer, when there is more choice, is the very thing they'll fight over when winter pickings are slim. Even so, very few food scraps end up in the compost anymore; instead these are fed to our animals who benefit from the nutrients while turning them into manure.

There are numerous things that can be foraged or grown in the garden to feed animals. Top left: Acorns. Mine come from a white oak species and are relished whole by my goats. Top right: Amaranth. I feed this ancient grain to goats & chickens, no threshing required. Bottom left: Broom corn, a type of sorghum, both seeds & leaves. Grain sorghum is an option too. Bottom right: Wild rose hips. I've also planted Rugosa roses for their larger, easier to pick hips.

Other things I offer: garden greens (collards, kale, turnip, beet, Swiss chard, dandelion), root crops (carrots, beets, turnips, mangels, parsnips, sugar beets, Jerusalem artichokes), winter squashes & pumpkins, sweet potato tubers & vines, blueberries, comfrey, melon & citrus rinds. These add roughage, as well as vitamins and minerals (see pages 219-223 for a more comprehensive list).

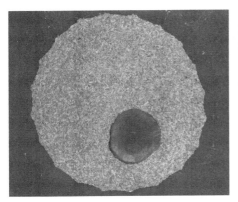

How and where to store our feeds has been a learning process. Above: grain stored in a vinyl trash can. To deter moths, chunks of fresh cut cedar are placed in the cans with the grain. Right: Our first attempt at a corn crib. It was made of welded wire fencing and two large plastic trays that Dan rescued from a dumpster. The problem was that our corn crib wasn't squirrel-proof.

The last challenge we've had to face has been storage. Now that we've grown it, where do we keep it, and how?

Of that first hay harvest, quite a bit mildewed from our ignorance about storing hay, and had to be put into the compost. We don't have a bailer so, after being scythe cut, it was allowed to dry in the field, raked into windrows, and hauled to the animal shed where it was heaped into old fashioned piles. We have learned to make sure it is completely dry before stacking it. Also to allow for air circulation beneath and around the hay. This can be done by putting it on pallets or a thick bed of dead branches. We now keep it in the carport to protect it from rain.

Wheat, if it isn't threshed in the field, must be stored on the stalk. The stalk is an important by-product because it is used for bedding or mulch as straw. Because we aren't set up for bulk threshing we've been storing the unthreshed wheat on our screened in front porch and feeding as needed.

I like to store grains is trash cans. In them, I can store either loose grain or 50 pound bags from the feed store. I can separate different kinds and mixes of feeds, and the cans are small enough to move easily. So far they have been rodentproof, but not mothproof. The best natural moth deterrent I've found is chunks of fresh cut cedar kept in the grain.

How do I know that my animals' nutritional needs are being met? The best indicator is the health and condition of the animals themselves. Also, I recently learned that I can have any feedstuff analyzed for its nutrient content through my state cooperative extension service. This not only gives me objective information about the quality of my feeds, but also is another indicator of how well our soil remineralization is succeeding. Cost for the test is nominal but the information is invaluable, especially for the major nutrients I am most concerned about such as protein and calcium.

As you can see, food self-sufficiency for animals seems complicated, even overwhelming. Yet it is not impossible; it is something that must be taken one step at a time. While success can be measured by how much less purchased feed we require, the best indicator is the animals themselves. When the goats have soft, sleek, shiny coats, and the chickens are busy scratching and clucking happily about their chicken business, I begin to see success in a different light. I begin to realize our goal to feed our animals from the land is the best choice, not because it enhances our self-reliance, but because it's the best choice for them.

NOTES

[1] *Texas Invasives* Invasives Database Pueraria montana var. lobata Kudzu Web. 14 Oct. 2013 <http://www.texasinvasives.org/plant_database/detail.php?symbol=PUMOL>

CHAPTER 8

ENERGY SELF-SUFFICIENCY

Riley by the woodstove. It can be used for cooking as well as heating.

Unlike food self-sufficiency, we've made very little progress toward energy self-sufficiency. Energy independence is a goal, but at this point it has not been the priority. We figure that, if push comes to shove, we can live without electricity, but we cannot live without food. Even so, we have observed, researched, and done what we can with a view, hopefully, of becoming energy self-reliant one day.

Like many folks, energy self-sufficiency is something we initially associated with being off-grid. As I began to research I learned that "the grid" can mean different things to different people. I always assumed "the grid" meant the electrical grid, so that being off the grid meant not purchasing power from the electric company. For some, off-grid has a broader meaning and includes other utilities such as water and sewage. Also it can mean the cultural grid, as in being totally incognito from all of society. Here, I will be using the term in reference to the electrical grid.

While electricity is the most familiar form of energy folks purchase, there are other common sources of energy for heating, water heaters, and cooking. That means I can be producing my own electricity, but still be dependent on someone else to meet part of my energy needs: propane, kerosene, home heating oil, gasoline or diesel to run a generator, even candles if I buy them at the store. Therefore I would say that it's possible to be off-grid (i.e. off the electrical grid) but not be completely energy self-sufficient. An example would be the Amish. While they don't use electricity, they often purchase other forms of energy for their homes. Being energy self-sufficient, on the other hand, means I'm meeting all of my energy needs myself.

Initially, we assumed energy self-sufficiency simply would be a matter of buying (or making) a system, either solar or wind, setting it up, telling the power company good-bye, and going on with life as usual. We knew this would be a few years down the road, so while we worked on repairs to the house and establishing other things on our homestead, we observed. Solar power meant having sun, and wind power meant having wind, so we paid attention to the sun and wind patterns in our area, as well as our electric usage. We paid attention to when the sun hit the house and when it became shaded. We observed where it rose and set in summer versus winter. We learned from which direction the wind blew, and when. As we observed, we did what we could toward energy independence.

The first thing we considered was our source for winter heat. The heating unit that came with the house was an outdoor unit, an old oil burning furnace packaged with an electric air conditioner. No one (realtors, inspector, nor us) noticed beforehand, but after we moved in, there was a rank oily smell in the house even when the unit wasn't in use. The home inspector had warned in his report that the heater was at the end of its service life. Also, he noted that that its chimney stack was too close to a window, which was not compliant with current building codes. Because of those things, I didn't feel safe using it.

We had lived with wood heat most of our married life, so this was the alternative of choice when we thought about replacing the furnace. In fact, one of the things we wanted when we looked at houses was a fireplace. Our plan was not to use the fireplace as is, but to use the chimney to install a wood heat stove. Because of that, we were pleased that this house did

Old oil burning heater with air conditioner. The tank was buried. The chimney venting outside the dining room window was not compliant with building codes.

indeed have a fireplace. What we didn't know was that the chimney was in very bad shape. This was not included on the inspection report, because home inspectors here typically defer fireplaces to experts. It didn't take an expert, however, to realize that the mortar in the attic chimney was barely holding the bricks together; it had long since deteriorated to sand. Dan could easily poke his finger into the chimney between the bricks. In the end, we had to tear the entire thing out. We started at the top and tore down the chimney and fireplace, all the way to the slab upon which it was built. In its place, we built an alcove and hearth for the woodstove (pg 108).

Our woodburning stove is a Woodstock Soapstone Fireview. Dan had previously gotten his hands on some literature from this company, and instantly we were sold. Soapstone has the wonderful ability to retain heat, which makes it an attractive feature in a wood heater. The soapstone will retain heat long after the fire is out, which we considered a major plus. On top of that, it had a catalytic combustor, which not only decreases pollution, but burns the smoke and gases to produce additional heat from the wood. When the catalytic combustor is engaged, very little smoke comes out the chimney. Unfortunately, these features mean this stove comes with a pretty price tag, too.

Our first renovation project was to tear down the chimney and fireplace, and make an alcove for our woodburning stove. Top left: Sliding chimney bricks off the roof. Top right: Building a hearth and wall shield. Cored (with holes) bricks allow air to enter the air gap behind the brick wall. Bottom left: Installing cement board ceiling and walls with vent cutouts. Bottom right: Completed alcove with stove installed.

We actually purchased this stove on faith. After we made an offer on the house, we requested and received current literature from the Woodstock company. Being early spring, lo and behold, they were having a huge clearance sale. The problem was that the ordering deadline was before our scheduled closing date for the house. Having already had a few ups and downs trying to buy this place, we didn't want to count our chickens before they were hatched and assume it was a done deal. The sellers had already balked, so we were not entirely certain the sale would go through. Yet, we did not want to lose out on such a good deal for the stove, so we ordered it. Fortunately, everything worked out, and we had not only the woodstove we wanted, but also a house to put it in.

That first winter our only heat source was the woodstove. That first winter we froze. Not that the woodstove didn't do its job, but it was an exceptionally cold winter and the house was poorly insulated. In addition, the stove is not centrally located; it is at the front of the house, in the living room. That meant that the back of the house, where the kitchen and bathroom are located, was terribly cold. I don't think it got above 45° F (7° C) in those rooms all that first winter, unless I was cooking. We ended up supplementing our wood heat with radiator type space heaters.

That first winter was an eye opener in terms of energy self-sufficiency. We had assumed we could utilize solar energy in the future, but that first winter we had no sun. Literally, for almost three months there was never a sunny day. It was a dark, frigid first winter in our new home, and left us realizing that solar may not be the entire answer of itself. Solar systems do generate electricity even on cloudy days, but we realized there could be significant limitations.

Springtime brought fierce winds; they were constantly blowing. Because of that we were hopeful about wind power. Then came summer, with hot blistery days and nary a breeze to stir them. As the windless days stretched into weeks, I researched wind power for our area and found an online wind resource map (now offline, see Appendix A for an alternative). I confess it was a little discouraging to discover that we live in a virtually zero wind resource area.

From my observations, I know this is not specifically true, but I do know that the only times it gets truly windy here are during storms and in the spring. Some spring days, it's so windy that the chickens won't venture far. They'll just stay huddled on the lee side of the goat shed. In summer we're lucky to get a gentle breeze. Over the course of the year, there is not enough wind to justify spending tens of thousands of dollars on a wind turbine that would only be productive a few weeks out of the year.

After our first full year on the homestead, we had our observations, but were no closer to energy self-sufficiency than before. The sun and wind realities of our area were one problem; money was the other. We ran out of money before we came up with answers to our energy self-sufficiency questions, and would not go into debt for it. As our second winter approached, we did not want a repeat of the first. We began to consider what we should do about keeping warm.

At the time, we had about $6,000 left in our homestead savings account. We spent many hours debating how to use it wisely. Had it not been for our sunless first winter here, we likely would have considered a solar powered system. As it was, we didn't. Instead we discussed whether it would be better to use the last of our savings on an HVAC (Heating, Ventilation, and Air-Conditioning) unit, or to invest it in insulation for our old house.

In our part of the country (the southeastern US), HVAC systems are common because they are heaters packaged with air conditioning units. In fact, because of our hot, humid summers, they are geared more toward the air conditioning part than the heating part. Having battled mold and mildew in humid houses in the South for many years, I knew that if we had an air conditioner, I would use it. I would set the thermostat high, but as long as we had the electricity to power it, I would use it.

One system we considered was geothermal (ground source heat pumps). I had great hopes in that, although these systems cost at least twice the money we had available. If we only needed electricity to operate the fan, and not condensers and heating elements, our electric usage and costs would be cut significantly. I thought, too, it might be feasible to generate enough of our own electricity to use it year around.

Dan wondered what it would take to install a geothermal unit ourselves. We learned that if we installed the system ourselves, we had just enough money to buy the unit. That was hopeful. The eye opener was when I eventually found an online DIY (do it yourself) geothermal forum. We learned that folks with geothermal systems only realized energy and monetary savings if they switched from a fossil fuel based system, such as home heating oil. This was because even geothermal furnaces utilized axillary heat sources (often electric) during the coldest winter months. That pretty much nullified our reasons for getting one in the first place. Something else we learned is that in real estate appraisals, geothermal systems do not increase the market value of the home. While we don't have plans for ever selling, this was still a surprise. In the end, we decided such an investment actually may not be an investment at all.

Right: Dan removes the exterior siding on the back porch to reveal blown-in insulation beneath.

Our house was built in the 1920s, before the invention of modern insulation. When we remodeled the kitchen, we found sheets of newspaper between the inner and outer walls. The blown-in cellulose type became popular in the 1970s, and at some point, was used to insulate our attic and walls. When we gutted the kitchen, we discovered places into which the insulation couldn't be blown, specifically under the windows and the diagonal bracing in the corners (pictured at right). We removed the old insulation and replaced it with the batting type. Between that and our new energy efficient windows, we have experienced a welcome difference in both comfort and energy savings.

In what seemed like a one step forward, two steps back move, we ended up using the last of our homestead savings on two things: a wood cookstove for the kitchen (one step forward), and an electric air source heat pump (two steps back). We decided on these, rather than putting the money into insulation, because lump sums of money rarely come our way. Insulation and other measures toward home energy efficiency could be paid for as we tackled them, one project at a time.

Dan first insulated all the ductwork for the heat pump himself, and then we had it installed. That was in October, right before our second winter in our house. Two months later, I finally found just the wood cookstove I wanted.

Actually I had been looking for a wood cookstove for awhile, mostly on Craigslist. There had been quite a few offered, most of them old and listed in the $500 - $600 range. We'd looked at a few of these, and although the owners thought they were in excellent condition, they had missing pieces, cracked parts, and loose fittings. They may have been lovely as antiques or decorative pieces, but they were in poor condition to use as functioning cookstoves.

One in particular didn't look as though it needed a lot of repair, so we looked into what it would cost to repair an old stove. The most common wood cookstoves for sale in our area were originally manufactured by Atlanta Stove Works. However, that company has been out of business for a long time, so there is no way to get replacement parts. Welding and metal fabrication are costly, so a $500 bargain likely would not be a bargain after all.

One day a Heartland Sweetheart wood cookstove showed up on Craigslist. When I first saw it, the asking price was $2500. That price seemed impossible to me, but there was also a Waterford Stanley (my dream stove) on Craigslist for $3000. That price seemed even more impossible. Still, I visited these ads often. After about a week, the price for the Waterford Stanley rose to $3500, but the Sweetheart eventually came down to $2000. Sweetheart stoves are still being manufactured in Canada by the Aga-Heartland company, so replacement parts and upgrades can be ordered. At that time, a basic model stove retailed for about $4000 new. This one included a water reservoir, rear heat shield, and floor protector, all of which added another $1000 to the value.

The heat shield is a must for a small kitchen like ours, as it drastically reduces the required clearance behind the stove to the wall. Without a heat shield, a minimum of 27 inches needs to be allowed between the stove and a combustible wall. With the shield, that clearance is reduced to just inches. Another plus was the hot water reservoir. These typically hold about five gallons of water, but are not standard on wood cookstoves. The free hot water provides additional savings in electricity.

Dan and I talked about the Sweetheart for some time. As badly as I wanted it, buying it would completely wipe out the remains of our house fund savings. Dan said that was what the money was for, so in the end, we decided to go see it. It was a good price for an important addition to our homestead. I admit that it took me several days to work up the courage to call to make an appointment. The ad was a month old by then, so I was pretty sure it had been sold. I was surprised that it wasn't, and made arrangements to see the stove. As advertised, it was in excellent condition. Not only did the price include the extras I mentioned above, but also all the pipe: double walled stove pipe, 12 feet of double walled insulated chimney pipe, storm collar, roof flashing, chimney cap, ceiling pipe

My Heartland Sweetheart Wood Cookstove with hot water reservoir. It is not only excellent to cook on, but keeps the back of the house warm, including the bathroom.

adapter, and attic insulation shield. All of this would cost an additional $1500 plus shipping to purchase new, but was included with the stove.

We bought it, loaded it up into the back of Dan's Chevy S-10 pick-up truck, and brought it home. We stored it in one of our outbuildings for over a year, until we were finally able to work on remodeling our kitchen.

The kitchen remodel was a huge project, but it made noticeable progress in the energy efficiency of our home. It was the first room in which we tore down the walls, made structural repairs (see photo of rotted rim joist on page 29), and added proper insulation. In addition we replaced the broken, drafty windows with new, energy efficient ones. To install the wood cookstove a big dip in the kitchen floor had to be leveled first. Dan tore out the exsisting floor, boxed it out, added extra floor support, and then embedded the brick-look cement floor protector into our new hardwood floor. All of these upgrades, plus the wonderful warm wood heat from the cookstove, turned one of the coldest rooms in the house into one of the warmest and most welcoming.

We have had the heat pump for about three years now, long enough to have a pretty good idea of what it costs us to use. During spring and autumn, when we do not use it at all, our average kilowatt hours are about 18 per day in our all-electric house. In summer, with the air conditioner thermostat set at 82° F (28° C), kWh usage jumps to 30 kWh average per day. That includes use of the electric stove for summer cooking and extensive canning. During the coldest winter months, using the heat pump without additional wood heat, we average about 50 kWh per day. This includes use of the electric clothes dryer and electric stove, but is largely due to the heat pump's auxiliary heat strips, which are also electric. When these turn on depends on outdoor temperature, humidity, and thermostat setting. For example, with the thermostat set at 68° F (20° C), the auxiliary heat strips kick in when the outside temperature is in the low 40s. Also they come on anytime I try to raise the thermostat setting more than a degree or two.

Besides being costly to run for heat, our air source heat pump does a poor job of keeping the house warm. This could have been remedied by installing auxiliary gas heat strips instead of the electric ones. This, in fact, is what salespeople tried to convince us to do. They warned that an air source heat pump becomes increasingly less efficient as the outside air temperature gets colder. This is true, of course, but we considered it would be our back up heat source, utilized (if at all) in chilly rather than cold weather. At best, the heat pump blows chilly air through the vents when the temperature drops into the 40s. Now that we have both the wood heater in the living room and the wood cookstove in the kitchen, we use the heat pump only on chilly days rather than all winter, and we are considerably more comfortable.

I should add that, even with wood heat, we are not entirely nonelectric in regards to heating our home. Ceiling fans in the living room and kitchen help push wood heat out of these rooms and into the rest of the house. This is not strictly necessary, but it does help. Also I should mention that there is one disadvantage to using a soapstone stove. While soapstone is wonderful at retaining heat, it takes awhile to heat up and, hence, heat the room or the house. That means that it isn't useful for short or quick fires for instant heat. The cast iron wood cookstove is much better for that. The soapstone stove, however, excels at producing longterm sustained warmth.

Kitchen tools I use frequently are kept handy on a utensil rack. I realized that the tools I reach for are out of habit, so I had to retrain myself to think of hand tools first. Keeping them visible and available helped with that. Hand tools are often quicker and simpler to set up, use, and clean up than electric gadgets and gizmos.

Many a night we have put a large log on a good coal bed, turned down the damper, and wakened to that same log still burning, and with a good coal bed to get a morning fire going quickly.

While all these things felt like a step in the right direction, they seemed insignificant in our overall journey toward becoming energy self-sufficient. Still, there were other small things we can do to "grid down," most of them lifestyle changes. I already used a solar and wind powered clothes dryer, also known as a clothesline. Most of my kitchen tools are hand tools. When my Kitchen Aid mixer died, I did not replace it. As I scour thrift stores, I find many manual devices to help with food processing, such as my King Kutter (pictured page 116), a $10 thrift store find. So much of using hand tools is habit, and, truly, many so called time saving gadgets take more time to pull out, set up, and clean after use, than doing the job by hand in the first place.

There were other steps we were taking as well, the insulation and energy efficient windows in the kitchen, for example. As we tackle the other rooms one by one, we will do the same. I found plans online for a solar oven and we discussed a second, outdoor wood cookstove for summer cooking and canning. Anything we can unplug when not in use we do. When one of the wood stoves is in use, we use either my French press coffee maker, or our stove top percolator. Both make much better coffee than my electric drip coffee maker. A windup clock in the kitchen works just fine to tell the time. Also I use smaller appliances instead of big ones when I can. My toaster oven pulls less wattage than my big electric oven, as does my bread machine if I'm only needing to make bread, or my crockpot rather than stove top for making sauce for canning.

We find all these changes really do add up and the following year we were able to cut our electric bill by more than half. For example, our November 2011 average was 33 kWh per day. We were able to bring it down to 15 kWh per day in 2012. That was used for: fluorescent light bulbs (used only as needed), 2 refrigerators (one energy star rated), 1 chest freezer (energy star rated), ceiling fans to circulate heat from the wood stoves, box fan at night for "white noise" (barking dogs and the occasional zooming, boom-boxing car), 2 LED night lights with switches to turn off during the day (the ones with light sensors often stayed on all day), computer,

"King Kutter" brand manual food processor. This was a $10 thrift store find and included five cone blades. It's easy to set up, does an excellent job, and is easy to clean up. In the above photo, I'm processing garden grown turnips for sauerruben.

occasional use of power tools, occasional use of electric dryer on rainy days, occasional use of electric stove when not cooking on the wood cookstove and for canning, occasional use of toaster oven, occasional use of bread machine, rare use of the electric skillet, rare use of a small hand mixer, rare use of crock pot or slow cooker (wood cookstove is excellent at this), occasional use of heat pump for mildly chilly days, vacuum cleaner a couple of times each week, television for watching DVDs several nights per week, radio when Dan's home from work, electric water heater for showers mostly (I use heated water from the cookstove water reservoir for washing dishes when I can),

My solar and wind powered clothes dryer. The umbrella design is an excellent space saver, but the short lengths of line make it trickier for hanging clothes and bed sheets.

and morning coffee for which I use the drip pot. We specifically avoided using the heat pump when the electric auxiliary heat strips turned on. When the wood cookstove was going, we did not need the electric heater in the bathroom because heat from the cookstove keeps it warm.

Other measures we took were to unplug things not in use (that teeny digital clock on the coffee pot is worthless anyway). We put the TV and DVD player on a surge protector so we can easily turn them off with a flip of a toggle switch. Also the computer is turned off at night.

The following month, December, our daily average kWhs increased as the weather turned colder. Still, 17.35 was significantly lower than the previous year's 47 kWh daily average. Weather, particularly rain, was a factor because it meant using my electric clothes dryer more. Also in that month we had a big remodeling project - the hall bathroom. We kept a small space heater going in that room to meet the minimum air and surface temperatures for various paints, caulks, and adhesives.

For the next several months the trend continued. We used more kWh than the previous month, but considerably less than the previous year. I

Our back porch serves as laundry and mud room plus summer and canning kitchen. It is a tremendous help for keeping heat and humidity from canning out of the house during our hottest months. In winter, it buffers wind and cold air.

felt, however, that we were at least able to make choices about how we were using our electricity, especially because of the repairs and updating we were doing on the house. We were using it as a tool, rather than a necessity.

At one point in time we discussed going nonelectric, as in living without any electricity at all, including an alternative energy source. Dan wasn't keen on this idea, however. Because it is theoretically possible to produce our own electricity, he didn't see a reason to do without it altogether. Much of our usage is nonessential, but we figure we need it for food storage, particularly the refrigerators and chest freezer. Second on my list after that is my computer! Even if we could generate just enough electricity to cover basics like these, it would be progress.

Even though we knew that sun and wind had limitations in our area, these seemed to be the only alternative energy possibilities offered to homeowners. With so many other homesteaders utilizing these, curiosity finally got the better of me and I decided to do some research on how feasible it might be for us to go solar.

Pricing, of course, depends upon usage, so this was the first thing I needed to know. I had a year's worth of electric bills, from which I could average my usage in kilowatt hours. Solar panels, on the other hand, are rated in watts, but how did that relate to the kilowatt hours I used? How would I know how many panels I might need? Simply comparing it to an appliance wattage chart wouldn't do, because my actual operation of these includes a time factor. I can turn on a 60 watt light bulb and use it for 3 minutes, or 3 hours. Obviously the actual amount of electricity used will not be the same. This is the difference between watts and kilowatt hours. The wattage is the amount of electricity needed for a device to operate; the kilowatt hours are the actual amount of electricity used to run it. I pay for what I use, so my electric bill specifies charges for kilowatt hours.

Many solar websites offer online calculators. Some wanted me to plug in the wattage for everything for which I used electricity: light bulbs, appliances, clock radios, water heater, HVAC, home entertainment system, computer, etc., and the anticipated operation time of each. That, in itself, was too much, so I found one (which has since disappeared) that started with my daily average kilowatt hours. After working through the steps, it estimated the would be $71,040 to cover 100% of our electric usage. The good news was that with the government solar energy rebate, the actual cost would be only $49,728 because I'd be reimbursed $21,312.

In our case, it may as well have been $49 million. Even if we'd had about $50K available, we'd still have to pay the entire cost upfront and then wait until tax time to get the rebate. Even at that, I figured it would take 42 years for the thing to pay for itself, assuming my electric bill remained the same. If I took out a loan to purchase the system, the additional interest would mean my energy self-sufficiency would cost me more than simply buying electricity from the power company.

There are some problems with this exercise. It uses averages, which while helpful, are not realistic. I may average 21 kWh per month, but that usage might range from 14 up to 28 kWh on any given day. Sizing my system for the 21 kWh daily average, would leave me relying on the electric company for above average days, or else I would need to install a larger system to address above average usage. To bring down the cost of the system, on the other hand, I might consider how to cut my usage as significantly as possible.

Besides the tax rebate, the other selling point is that the power company will buy back any excess electricity one produces (not mentioned is that this is at a much lower rate than what it costs the consumer to purchase it). Unfortunately, when the grid goes down, so do all grid-tied systems, unless they include backup batteries or a backup generator. On top of that, I learned that the government rebates are only given for grid-tied systems. Those of us looking toward energy independence wouldn't be eligible for a rebate.

I blogged about this and got some really good feedback from off-grid readers; the number of solar panels, for example. My estimate for a grid-tied system recommended enough solar panels to power our real time usage. An off-grid system needs only enough panels to keep one's batteries charged. Other factors include the type of inverter and its distance from the panels, wire size, how it's wired, and the voltage of the system into which it is tied. For an A/C powered home, energy is lost converting the D/C power coming from the batteries. Maintenance is a necessity too. Solar panels have a lifespan, as do batteries, and generators require

We erected a privacy fence not only to define our backyard, but also as a place to stack and store firewood. Wood is a sustainable energy source, as long as new trees are planted to replace the ones cut down.

maintenance and sometimes repair. As the components of the system age, the potential problems and repair requirements increase. When any one part of the system is down, the entire system is down. These are the kinds of things I learned from folks who actually are off-grid.

I did a similar exercise with wind energy, and had about similar results in terms of cost and effectiveness. As with solar, I learned more about the real world problems with wind power from off-grid bloggers than from the websites set up to promote energy alternatives. For example, without sustained winds, results will be poor. Some advertising claims that as little as 10 mph is adequate, but the fine print will disclose that this will only generate enough electricity to power a florescent light bulb or two for a couple of hours. Actually what they are referring to is called "cut-in speed", the speed at which the turbine will begin to turn. "Rated output speed" is the minimum sustained wind speed needed for the turbine to generate its designated rated power. Typically this is 25 to 35 mph. "Cut-out speed" (usually between 45 and 80 mph) is the wind speed at which the turbine reaches the limits of its alternator. At the cut-out speed, a braking mechanism causes the turbine to shut down. This is a safety feature to protect the turbine from damage, but also means that in very high winds, electricity will not be produced.

Wind speeds between the cut-in speed and the rated speed will produce varying amounts of electricity. This might not be bad for a grid-tied system, but for an off-grid system, this can be a problem. This can be resolved by installing the turbine on a tower which can reach sustained winds, usually a minimum of 100 feet (30 meters). Unfortunately, this height often is prohibited by local codes.

There are other considerations, such as noise and maintenance costs. Variable wind and high gusts cause wear and tear on the turbine, and must be taken into account. Also there is the potential to drain power from the battery bank when the turbine is not producing electricity, unless the system has a blocking diode. Unfortunately, things like this are not always disclosed in the sales pitch.

For Dan and me, the bottom line was twofold. Because our sun and wind resources are less than adequate, and because these systems are so expensive, neither seems truly feasible for us. While keeping a generator to charge a battery bank seems the way to go, we need to consider how to feed the generator. This is the question we currently ponder and for which hard information is sketchier. Research on other alternative energies is limited because government subsidies go to the solar and wind industries.

Hydro is a possibility for those living near water, which, unfortunately, we don't. Other than that we've read sketchy accounts of using methane, biomass, wood gasifiers, biodiesel, and hydrogen, but without enough information to answer practical questions regarding building and implementing such systems.

If I were asked to summarize what we've learned about energy independence so far, I'd say several things. Firstly, it is a complex and expensive goal to reach. Secondly, its success primarily will depend on our lifestyle. We live in a flick of the switch society, and I suspect most of us think we do well to remember to turn off the light when we leave the room. The reality of producing one's own electricity and being energy independent is akin to living on a strict budget with no credit card. The day's activities must be determined by the amount that's stored in the battery bank, plus the potential to create more on that particular day. Sometimes choices must be made: would I rather use my Kitchen Aid mixer to knead a loaf of bread or run the washing machine? Would I rather use my power saw or my electric drill? If my system doesn't meet my needs, I have to make choices: increase the size of the system and add more batteries, learn to decrease my usage with nonelectric tools and appliances, or learn how to live without.

I confess that energy self-sufficiency is a goal that, at this time, seems beyond our reach. Not that we don't have the desire, but we definitely don't have the means, and as we approach what most consider retirement age, I wonder if we have the time. If we'd started homesteading in our 20s or 30s, we'd likely be far beyond all this now. That does not mean, however, that we give up on the goal. It means that we accept the reality of our situation and take whatever steps we can. I admit that some days, like the day we had our heat pump installed, it actually seemed as though we were going backwards. The reality is that a self-sufficient homestead takes years to develop and many small steps to achieve. As with all things, it's one step at a time.

CHAPTER 9

WATER SELF-SUFFICIENCY

Three week old baby chicks drink from a chick waterer.

During my back-to-the-land days in the Ozark Mountains, having water meant damming up a mountain spring and gravity feeding fresh spring water to a faucet in the outdoor kitchen via a hose. Spring houses used to be common in bygone days, especially on farms with dairy animals. Milk houses in particular would take advantage of a spring's icy cold waters to keep milk fresh in the days before refrigeration. I had off-grid friends in Tennessee who kept the milk from their cow fresh by piping icy spring water through an old chest freezer, where they kept their jars of milk.

There aren't many springs to be had in our southern Appalachian foothills, or at least none were ever mentioned in real estate ads when we were looking at land. Likely they are still to be found in some undeveloped areas, but with land prices as high as they are, Dan and I instead looked for a place with an existing dwelling. That meant either a well or city water rather than a spring. We particularly hoped for a well.

Over the years we've lived with both city water and well water, and have learned the benefits and problems of each, including storing water for emergency situations. The place we now homestead is right outside of town and has city water. I'll allow that it's convenient and works when the grid is down because we don't need electricity for the pump. We don't have to worry about problems with water pressure or maintaining the pump. We don't have to worry about running out of water when I forget to turn off the sprinkler and use up all the water in the tank.

City water, on the other hand, comes with a monthly bill, chemicals, and other contaminants. These affect not only taste and smell (ours is terrible on both counts), but also what we have to ingest. Well water, on the other hand, varies in taste according to location. The best we ever had was when we lived in central Florida.

Nowadays well water is usually accessed with an electric pump. That means that if one is on-grid and the electricity goes down, guess what, no water. We learned that a 55 gallon drum of stored water lasts a family of 4 only a couple of days if carefully used, and not counting flushing toilets. Well water is not necessarily free of chemicals and contaminants either; it depends on the location of the groundwater source. When we had well water with copper plumbing, we found sediment and pipe corrosion to be higher due to the water's mineral content. Still, if I had a choice, I'd choose well water over city water any day.

We know that when our home was first built in the 1920s, there was a well. We just don't know for certain where it is yet. Old surveys don't show things like that. Our neighbor's was where his driveway is now. He discovered it when it created a small sinkhole that tried to swallow up one of their cars. He had hoped to use it for watering their garden, but alas, it was dry. Whether or not ours would be serviceable remains to be seen. Like so many other things, finding the old well is a future project for our to-do list.

We sometimes consider having a new well dug. Because we do have water, this is not a priority, but it does remain on our "hope to do someday" list. Whether or not we'll actually do it will depend primarily on cost; county ordinances are another factor.

As with most of our other projects, we know that we could keep the construction cost down if we did the labor ourselves. The idea of hand digging a well, however, is a daunting task. We've done no serious research toward this end, but, as I am always on the lookout for resources for our home library, I did find and purchase *Hand Dug Wells and Their Construction* by S.B. Watt and W.E. Wood. Written primarily for well construction in third world countries, it is nonetheless thorough.

There are a number of reasons why we'd like to have our own well. Firstly, because it fits better into our concept of self-reliance. This ties into water availability. While a municipal water system is not subject to electrical outages, availability can be effected in other ways. It may or may not seem far-fetched to entertain the possibility of a terrorist attack on our local water system, yet problems with contamination do arise from time to time, usually because of breaks in water mains or flooding problems due to weather. It's not uncommon in our area for citizens to be advised to boil their tap water before drinking it or using it for cooking.

Another concern is purity. While well water can be contaminated, it is not loaded with chlorine and fluoride. Neither is it likely to contain traces of pharmaceutical drugs, which enter the municipal water system through human waste, nor industrial contaminants.

Never underestimate the many uses of water. This Delaware hen and her friend took turns cooling their feet in a nearby watering dish one sweltering summer day.

Lastly is cost. While wells are expensive to dig and do require maintenance, they are not subject to periodic rate increases. We currently have city water and a septic system. When we lived with city sewage, we obviously paid for the additional service. At the time, the cost was roughly double that of the water portion of the bill. When I inquired as to how these were calculated, I was told sewage charges were based on water usage. I confess this annoyed me a bit, because it meant I was paying for sewage on water for that didn't go down the drain and therefore wasn't being treated in the municipal water facilities: watering the garden or washing the car for example. I don't know if the same is true elsewhere, but it was certainly true where we lived at the time.

Our septic system, on the other hand, requires maintenance and can have things go wrong. Routine maintenance includes being pumped out periodically, as well as making sure the system has the proper bacteria to break down the waste. Bleach and other chemical cleaners can kill these, so I'm always on the lookout for products labeled septic safe. According to M. G. Kains in his classic *Five Acres and Independence*, it is possible to have a system which never needs pumping out[1]. At least, this was the author's experience. His book was first published in 1935 and I've wondered about that. What is the key to owning a maintenance-free septic system? Was it the way in which it was constructed? Or perhaps because there were no modern day cleaners and chemicals going down the drain and into the tank?

About a year after we bought our place we had problems and had to have a new leach field put in. Also called a drain field, or finger

A year after we bought the place, we discovered a huge puddle which turned out to be a problem with the septic tank. A new leach field had to be dug.

system, this is the underground area that soaks up the water draining from the septic tank. Because it is located underground, the surface soil remains dry. If muddy areas or puddles appear, it means there is a problem. This is exactly what we discovered after I cleared away all the brush in the area, a permanently muddy spot in the vicinity of the buried septic tank. Dan dug out around it and discovered that there was no drain pipe for the overflow. The solution included putting in a new leach field.

Alternatives to either city sewage or a septic system include composting toilets and greywater recycling systems. I could include an outhouse, and have lived with outhouses in the past. Although outhouses have no levers or plumbing, they still require maintenance. They do fill up, must be relocated on occasion, and they do smell. Wood ash is a sustainable way to deter flies, although usually barn lime is used. The worst part is needing to make a frigid trip at 2 a.m. in the middle of January, when it's sleeting out and the path is icy. And the battery in the flashlight is dead. Ask me how I know. The alternative to that scenario is the chamber pot. However, this ancient ancestor of the modern bed pan somehow appealed less than going to the outhouse in the middle of the night.

Dan and I took a brief look at composting toilets, but dismissed the idea after that. The concept is excellent, but they are outrageously expensive, not only the unit but also installation, which requires a composting area. They are not maintenance free, and as with garden composting systems, the conditions must be correct to aerobically produce compost. Carbonaceous material must be added and the temperature kept optimum, often with an electric heating element. Lastly there is the chore of clean out. At least all that was true of the ones I researched.

In the end, it made more sense for us to replace our old full flush toilets with new low flush models. These typically use less than half the water that the older toilets use. Early low flush toilets were extremely inefficient and could require two flushes per use. Unfortunately, they still carry that reputation but have been much improved in recent years. The key is in the flushing mechanism, i.e. one that actually works with one flush and without electricity. Ours accomplish this with 1.28 gallons, as opposed to the standard 3.5 gallons. While this still goes into the septic system, we figured it was a start.

For our drinking and cooking water we bought a water filter. Our municipal tap water was a strong motivator for this. Some days it smells so strongly of chlorine that turning on the faucet makes me want to gag. The options for water filtration are either individual units or whole house filters. If we once again had well water, Dan would have wanted a whole house filter because of the pipe corrosion we'd experienced in the past. With city water, however, we felt our concern should focus on water for drinking and cooking. Filtering water that goes down the drain did not make sense, especially when the filters have to be replaced periodically.

The factors we considered were contaminants filtered out, longevity of the filtering elements, energy consumption, ease of maintenance, and price. A Berkey best met our circumstances, needs, and budget constraints. The clincher was not the sales pitch, but the fact that it is a common unit on the mission field, where it is being used in primitive conditions to provide potable water from sources none of us would otherwise dream of drinking.

In addition to the water filter, we made one other major purchase for our water needs: a water heater. The water heater that came with our house was a very old lowboy electric tank model, located in the crawlspace. The home inspection report indicated that it was reaching the end of its service life, so we knew we would need to replace it soon. Because of our sunless first winter here, we did not consider a solar water heater as a primary solution. What we did look into were tankless water heaters.

Tankless water heaters were all the rage, and originally that's what we planned to install too. The first thing we did was go to the home improvement store to price them. After talking to a sales associate and doing our own research, however, we ended up with a plain, old fashioned non-digital, non-computerized, conventional storage tank water heater.

Why? There were several reasons. The benefit of a tankless heater is that once warmed up, it provides an endless supply of hot water. For a large family needing lots of hot water for showers, baths, laundry, and the dishwasher, unlimited hot water would definitely be an attractive feature. I already do laundry in cold water, so we only need hot water for washing dishes (done by hand), showers for just two of us, and an occasional bath. For us, having unlimited hot water was not a strong selling point.

The appeal for us was in energy savings, but here's where the connection between sales pitch and reality becomes murky. The biggest savings are seen with gas tankless heaters, typically a $6 to $9 savings per month. Electric models show less savings, probably because of the amount of electricity needed to fire up the heating element. Any savings are offset, however, because tankless models are very expensive to install (double or more the cost of conventional water heaters), and require more maintenance than conventional models. The death knell, however, was that they waste considerably more water before hot water comes from the tap. Typical estimates were two minutes before hot water began to flow.

The old low boy water heater was located in the crawlspace. It didn't take up room in the house but was awkward to get to and a tight fit to get out. In fact, it got stuck in the doorway. I could imagine the newspaper headlines the next day, "Man Trapped in Crawlspace by Water Heater." Removing the door sill did the trick.

In the end, the best choice for us was a conventional tank storage water heater. No, it isn't trendy, but it best suited our hot water needs and our budget. Plus, it can be incorporated into a solar water heating system as a hot water storage tank, which a tankless water heater cannot.

A solar hot water heater is a relatively simple, inexpensive way to utilize the sun's heat and at this point, would be supplementary for us. This is another future project and because our mild winters are not freeze-free, will require research to determine the best type of system for us: batch, which uses a storage tank, or drainback or closed loop, with anitfreeze and a possibly a heat exchanger. Do we want a direct pump or a no-pump thermosiphon system? These are the kinds of choices we need to research and consider because even a simple system needs to be built properly and requires maintenance.

Drawing hot water from my wood cookstove's 5 gallon reservoir.

Huge rain puddles from roof run-off got us thinking about rainwater collection.

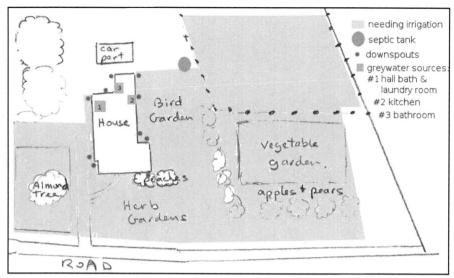

To assess our potential for water conservation we made a sketch of the house and areas we would need to irrigate. Our water sources include rainwater and greywater from kitchen, laundry room, and bathroom sinks, tub, and showers.

Water conservation, both greywater recycling and rainwater collection, is a step toward water self-sufficiency as well as stewardship. These have a number of benefits including relying less on freshwater from the tap, and reducing waste water entering the septic (or sewer) system. Of particular interest to us is irrigation; our hot summer dry spells have meant a doubling or more of our water bill when I water the garden. We could minimize that by utilizing these two water resources.

While both rainwater and greywater recycling seem simple in concept, implementing them is not so simple. There is no one-size-fits-all plan for either one. They require research, assessment, knowledge accumulation, consideration of local building codes, and careful planning. Care must be taken to not create more problems while trying to solve others.

We started with rainwater catchment. We found used, 275 gallon food grade "totes" on Craigslist for a reasonable price, so Dan purchased four. Their metal cages stack well, so that two together can collect and store more than 500 gallons of rainwater, plus, we hoped, would provide the pressure we would need to irrigate the farthest areas of the garden. We chose a back corner gutter as the place to start. Placement of the tanks was tough, because we didn't want to block the window, and putting them at the corner of the house would block the path to the garden between the house and carport.

Our first rainwater collection set-up was experimental.

The tanks came with shut-off valves, so Dan added a hose bib to the bottom tank, to which we can attach an ordinary garden hose. To prevent leaves and dirt from entering the tanks, he added a clean-out plug. Initial rainfall washes debris off the roof and into the clean-out tube. Once the tube is full, water flows into the tanks so that only clean rainwater enters them. The end cap can be unscrewed to empty the drain pipe tube into a bucket.

That small section of roof measures 15 by 7.5 feet or 112.5 square feet. Would it be enough to fill our tanks? Our curiosity was obliged that first night with a third of an inch of rain. This gave us two inches in the bottom tank. It was an exciting sight to behold. From subsequent rains we have learned that one inch of rainfall gives us 50 gallons in the tanks. That means it takes 5.5 inches of rain to fill one tank to its 275 gallon capacity.

Initially, we considered this set-up to be experimental. We've learned that many of our projects need adjustments and tweaking as we go along, so it's much easier to expect them. Dan was not surprised then, when there was a leak at the connector hose between the top and bottom tanks.

Top left: Clean-out plug. Debris is washed from the roof and into the plug, which can be cleaned as needed. Top right: Clean water flows into the top tank via a down-sloping pipe. Bottom left: Connector with shut-off valve. Bottom right: Hose bib fitted to the valve on the bottom tank. I can hook up a garden hose when I need to irrigate.

Initial solutions were to try various types of caulk to plug the leak. We had to wait until it rained again to test each sealant, but in the end, none worked. Even waterproof caulks state they are not for underwater use, or as in this case, in constant contact with water. In addition, there was the pressure from the water in the tank so that the leak remained. For awhile, it looked as though the entire project might be bust.

What Dan wanted, was a flanged fitting, but we couldn't find anything locally, nor online for a decent price. Finally, on a trip to Iowa, he found something at Bomgaars that he hoped would work: a threaded flanged fitting for the outside of the tank. This screws into a gland nut and washer on the inside.

Once installed, we had to wait until it rained to see if this worked. The following week we had an inch of rain which began to fill the top tank. The water level remained steady - leak fixed!

The last thing we have to do is to add an overflow to the system. I should mention, too, that there are other problems with our particular set-up. The totes, being translucent, will allow algae growth. The solution here is to paint them. Paint will also protect the tanks from sunlight. PVC breaks down in sunlight, leaching carcinogens into the water. In addition, we do not have the best kind of roof for rainwater collection. A metal roof would be much better than the asphalt shingles we had put on. In fact, we might have had a metal roof if our homeowners insurance company hadn't pressured us to get the roof replaced. If we'd had more time, we would have installed a metal roof ourselves at a fraction of the cost of having it done professionally. After much discussion, we settled for what we could afford; conventional roofing shingles plus labor.

On the plus side, our mild winters mean we do not have to worry about the tanks freezing. The water's thermal mass retains enough heat to keep it from freezing when temperatures dip below 32° F (0° C) at night.[2] If we had sustained freezing temperatures, however, we would need freeze protection.

All things considered, it was very encouraging to see how much rainwater we collect from that small roof. With more tanks to collect from the rest of the roof, we have the potential to collect water for irrigation, toilet flushing, and laundry. Rainwater could even be used for cooking, bathing, and drinking, providing proper materials and filtration were used.

We still have two more totes, but after reading Art Ludwig's *Water Storage*, Dan would like to try his hand at making a rainwater collection tank with ferrocement. Ferrocement is considered one of the best materials for water tank construction, but this will be another future project.

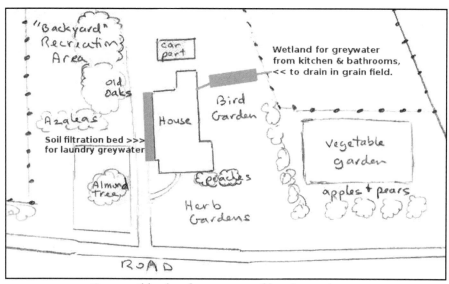

One possible plan for greywater filtration and usage

Another of Art Ludwig's books, *Create an Oasis with Greywater*, will be our primary resource when we add a greywater recycling system. I've made sketches of several possibilities, the current top contenders are illustrated on this page. We have two potential areas, one from the kitchen and bathrooms (sinks, tub, and showers), the other from the laundry room. A wetland is one idea for kitchen and bathroom greywater drainage as in the sketch above.

Possible greywater soil filtration bed with privacy fence & pergolas to shade windows. Laundry would be the source of the greywater. I would plant deciduous vines to climb up the pergola trellises, to offer summer shade but winter sun.

For laundry greywater, I'd like to build a raised soil filtration bed alongside the house. Pergolas would frame the bedroom windows and in the bed, I'd plant deciduous vines to grow up pergolas. This will shade the windows from the afternoon summer sun, yet allow sunshine to fall upon the windows during winter. A valve will allow us to direct greywater into the filtration bed, or into the septic tank, depending on rainfall amounts, or to periodically flush the system. Because greywater is not allowed to stand, freeze protection is not necessary. Besides whatever heat it contains as it drains from the house, microbial activity generates heat as it biodegrades, so that freezing is rare.[3]

These projects are still future, but by having a plan we are able to make plumbing repairs and upgrades with them in mind. We don't want to have any reworking to do when we get the systems installed. Mapping and sketching not only records our ideas, but ensures that Dan and I are both visualizing the same thing (which is not always the case).

Plans for greywater irrigation also must take the plants into account. Because waste water from laundry, dishwashing, and bathing is no longer potable, is not recommended for salad greens or root crops which will be eaten raw. Nor is it recommended for use with a sprinkler system. In addition, care must be taken with household and personal care products going down the drain. Biodegradability comes to mind. Although some of the chemicals in these products may be biodegradable and considered safe for humans, they can still be toxic to plants. Two such chemicals are sodium (salts) and boron (borax). Sodium is typically found as sodium lauryl sulfate, a surfactant. It is used to make bubbles and foam in liquid soaps, liquid dishwashing detergents, shampoos, shower gels, bubble baths, even toothpaste. Boron as borax is considered a natural cleaning agent and is an important micronutrient for plants. Unfortunately, it can be toxic to them if allowed to build up in the soil.

Another problem is that most soaps and detergents raise the greywater's pH, making it more alkaline. If the greywater is to be used for irrigation, this will be a problem for acid loving plants. Alkalinity is a characteristic of not only commercial soaps and detergents, but homemade ones as well. While the pH of handcrafted bar soaps neutralizes as they age, homemade laundry detergent is primarily two highly alkaline ingredients, washing soda and borax. One practice that helps the alkalinity problem, is to flush the greywater system periodically with rainwater. In addition, there are a number of greywater friendly products on the market. When our first greywater project becomes imminent, I will research these as well as homemade alternatives.

In what other ways do we conserve water? If I need hot water from the faucet, I collect the cold water into a pitcher while waiting for the hot water to flow. This is used either to water plants or it goes into the washing machine if I'm about to do laundry. Cooking and canning waters are allowed to cool and used on plants as well. Before we bring fresh water to our animals, the leftover water in the buckets is used to refill birdbaths or poured onto thirsty plants.

Unlike food or energy, water, usually, is not thought of as a goal for self-sufficiency. Because so many current discussions revolve around purity and availability, mostly it is thought of in terms of conservation. Particularly, the term "global water crisis" is thrown around, but I think that is a misnomer, because there are no global solutions to these problems. My conserving water in the southeastern United States is not going to make it more available in a drought-plagued area on another continent. My concerns must focus on my regional water problems, which typically include an annual summer dry spell. I cannot grow water like food, nor make water like electricity, but I can take action to make sure it is available and adequate for my needs. That includes being responsible in our water usage, because that is what stewardship is all about.

NOTES

[1] M. G. Kains, *Five Acres And Independence* (NY: Dover Publications, 1974) 75.

[2] Art Ludwig, *Water Storage: Tanks, Cisterns, Aquifers, and Ponds* (Santa Barbara: Oasis Design, 2011) 73.

[3] Art Ludwig, *Create an Oasis with Greywater* (Santa Barbara: Oasis Design, 2011) 126.

CHAPTER 10

OBSTACLES

Which is the obstacle, the fence or the cat? The answer depends upon point of view.

If you were to ask homesteaders about the obstacles they face, I think several things would be on the list: shortages of knowledge, resources, skills, tools, time, and especially money. Even if we have enough money to buy land, we quickly realize how expensive it's going to be to get a working homestead going. Even so, I'd say there is a bigger obstacle that stands in the way whether we have enough money or not. It's an obstacle of which most folks aren't even aware. It is their worldview, or mindset. By this I mean one's expectations about how things ought to be, about life and society as we are used to them. It's our attitude, particularly, about what we have, what we need, and how we get it. It's our mental image about cultural and lifestyle standards, of how life ought to be lived, how things ought to work.

The early inhabitants of the New World, both Native Americans and European immigrants, had to be largely self-reliant in meeting their needs. This affected what they did and how they did it. They had to rely on the land and the work of their hands to live and to survive. They could trade, barter, or sell, but within a local context. The industrial revolution changed all that. It changed people's ability to obtain goods, and it changed how they obtained them. Also it changed society's ideas about the value of those goods, as well as the values of labor and money. Folks now had to work for money in order to live and enjoy life. The value of a job was no longer in the satisfaction it brought, but in how much money it could earn. While many would say we gained a lot thanks to technology, many would say we lost something as well. Something very important.

Today, many folks are concluding that the modern way of life is too complicated and less fulfilling than they feel it can be. I think this feeling is at the root of the homesteading movement and why so many folks are turning toward what they hope will be a simpler life. They want to be involved in the basic processes of life because there is a sense of purpose and satisfaction in that. They want to enjoy what they're doing for the doing's sake, as well as meeting their own needs. They are not necessarily striving to find something new; rather there is a sense of returning to something old, returning to the thing that we instinctively know the modern world has lost.

What we lost was the agrarian way of life. It is not a specifically rural way of life, but one that is based on the land and what the land can provide. Today, we look, instead, to what technology and our investments can provide. Agrarian economics is based in agriculture. Today's economics are based on consumerism and ever-increasing profits. This has profoundly shaped cultural attitudes, expectations, and perceptions of the world, of its resources, our fellow humans, their purpose, and how these things interrelate. This is important to understand because I think our worldview or mindset is key to successful homesteading. Our mindset shapes our goals and how we go about meeting them. It is the basis upon how we judge our success.

At the core, both of these mindsets are about our relationship with the land, or the earth if you will. They are about whether or not we have the right to own it and how we interact with it. The question at the heart of it is, are we a part of the natural world which meets our needs as we exercise stewardship, or are we a separate entity which simply uses, controls, and capitalizes on creation's resources?

Agrarian thinking partners with the land. Security to the agrarian is in the land and the skills needed to make it productive through work, experience, and common sense. Because of their tie with the natural world, agrarians understand that there are uncertainties in life. This is why agrarianism is community focused. Agrarians believe it is a social responsibility to help others. It seeks to make a living, not a fortune, and its life goals are based on personal productivity and contentment. Trustworthiness is based on one's character, not one's credit rating. Money is basically a tool to meet needs. The goal of life is contentment and personal productivity. The concepts of recycling, reusing, sustainability, self-reliance, and self-sufficiency are natural extensions of the lifestyle, not individual activities which must be striven for.

The little ditty:

> Use it up,
> wear it out,
> make it do,
> or do without.

is an example of the agrarian mindset.

The modern, industrial age mindset, on the other hand, is based on consumerism and accumulating wealth. It is exemplified by the following clichés:

> time is money
> quick and easy
> buy now, pay later
> I'm worth it

A consumer/profit mindset considers land an investment. Its knowledge base and source of authority is science and expertise. Its source of security is in investments, portfolios, net worth, jobs, economic growth, the stock market, building starts, consumer confidence, etc. This mindset might tout the virtues of recycling and sustainability, but in reality expendable is good. Disposable is good, instant gratification is good, product dependency is good, debt is good, anything that increases profits is good and desirable. The consumer/profit mindset thinks of people in terms of demographics rather than communities. It thinks globally, not locally, because more people means more profit. There is no sense of social responsibility here; that's the government's job. There is no accountability because the end justifies the means. One's trustworthiness is not based on character, but credit rating. Money is not seen as a tool, but as a measure of success, personal importance, and power. The goal in life is to accumulate and secure one's wealth. This is seen as the key to being happy.

At one time, it was possible to close a deal on a handshake. A man's word was considered his bond. In our modern world that now seems naively old-fashioned. In our modern way of doing business, even a signature on a contract is merely a ritual. Lying is no longer considered a sin, but socially acceptable, even expected.

Wendell Berry, in his essay "Three Ways of Farming in the Southwest", cites an incident[1] at the 1979 World Hunger Conference at the University of Arizona, which beautifully illustrates the differences between these two worldviews. When asked whether traditional, local forms of agriculture should be encouraged as a means of helping alleviate world hunger, the panel's response was no. The way to solve world hunger was to develop cash economies so that people could have jobs and buy food.

Some may see these worldviews as modern and progressive versus old-fashioned and nostalgic and wonder, "What's wrong with thus-and-such?" After all, even agrarians consume things and money is necessary to buy things that can't be produced at home. That is true. However, it's neither the consumer part nor the money part that is the problem. The problem is in how we view these things. Both mindsets describe a means to an end. The question should not be which is right or wrong, but rather, is the modern mindset a reflection of true progress? Does it signify a more sophisticated approach to life and world matters? Has it actually solved social problems, or created more of them?

I have made an interesting observation from readers' comments to my blog posts and from reading their homestead blogs as well. It is that despite our different social, cultural, religious, and political backgrounds and ideologies, homesteaders have one significant thing in common: a sense that modern thinking and the way of life it fosters is flawed. That it's forgotten things that are important. That it can provide neither true security nor a sense of individual life purpose. That the social model it has created is doomed to fail.

How does this effect us on a personal level? Consider value. What do you think gives a thing value? Is it how rare it is? How much for which it sells? How much someone else says it's worth? For its potential to make money? Or, is its value based on how much others need or want it? I daresay most folks in Dan's and my shoes would look at our home improvements and ask themselves, "how long before thus and such pays itself off?" Or, "how much of a return can we get when we sell the house?"

As homesteaders, I think our view of value needs to be different. It is part of the mindset that can make or break our sense of success. Dan's and my goal, which I think is a typical one for homesteaders, is to meet more of our own needs through our relationship with the land. That could be extended somewhat, to secondarily meeting them through our relationship with like-minded folks in our local community. I'm going to suggest that our success will hinge, in part, on how we perceive value.

Let's take chickens as an example. Every homesteader, rural or urban, thinks about getting chickens. One of the first things we typically do is calculate the cost. This is compared with the price of eggs at the grocery store. If we want chickens for meat, we can figure that in too. In my case, I included the manure for compost and the ability to produce replacement chickens. After all that, the question we inevitably reflect on is, which

Chickens often give us our first glimpse into homestead economics.

is cheaper, keeping chickens or buying eggs? We try to determine the value of our endeavor by what it will cost us versus what we can recover.

At some point in our chicken deliberations, we entertain the idea of selling our surplus eggs to offset our expenses. No problem with that, but it finally occurred to me that, for what I was claiming my goals to be, I was asking the wrong questions. The question I ought to focus on was not, "can I make the chickens pay for themselves and maybe make a profit to boot?" The question ought to be, "do I want to have a self-sustaining source of eggs, meat, compost, and chickens?" If the answer is yes, then the cost comparison becomes largely irrelevant. If I have the money, I get the chickens and work toward feeding them from my own land. Here, their value is based on my need and how well they help me attain my goal, not whether I can get my so called money's worth from them.

Another example. Let's say I have an old farm tractor "worth" $2000, and you have a freshened dairy cow "worth" $1600. I need milk for dairy products to feed my family. You need to grow more grain and harvest more hay for your cows. We each need what the other has. A consumer/profit based trade would assume, "you still owe me $400". Whether or not the trade could take place would depend upon whether or not the cow's owner had an additional $400 in cash or goods to complete the transaction. If not, neither party would have their needs met. A need based trade, however, might make the trade as-is and call it even-steven.

What I'm suggesting is that money is not the only standard by which we can set value. This was a major shift in thinking that occurred after the industrial revolution. Before that, barter was more common and value was set more by how well a thing fulfills a needs or helps meet a goal.

I realize most folks won't want to do it that way. That's simply not the way things are done and money is, after all, a convenient way of setting value. This points out another problem and leads to another example.

If I have a rare book that an appraiser states is worth $1,000 but nobody wants it, is it really worth $1,000? I could theoretically starve to death because I wouldn't part with it for less than $1,000. If someone was finally willing to pay $500 for it, is it still worth $1,000? The original owner might think so and assume they'd been cheated. I'd say it is only worth $1,000 if the new owner can sell it for that. If not, then it's only worth what the next buyer is willing to pay. In other words, value is arbitrary, and I would suggest that ultimately, a thing's value is only what someone else is willing to pay for it. A real life example is the 2008 mortgage crisis, where many folks suddenly found they could only sell their homes for considerably less than what they owed on them.

Another example of the mindset I'm talking about is exemplified in the movie, *It's A Wonderful Life* with James Stewart and Donna Reed. In the story, the Baileys were interested in helping folks own their own homes, more so than they were in large profits. They lived comfortably but modestly, and were willing to sacrifice to help meet peoples' needs. Mr. Potter, on the other hand, cared more about profit than people, even lying and stealing to get what he wanted. Of course he was the bad guy, and in the end we all cheered when things worked out for George Bailey. We might think of this as nothing more than a Christmastime feel-good movie, but it illustrates the real life viewpoints I'm talking about.

Now, I'm not trying to minimize the reality of money, nor am I suggesting that it is possible to do away with it. What I am saying, is that there is more than one way of looking at it. It can be viewed as wealth, security, and power, or as one of a variety of tools in a toolkit. Unfortunately, economics has become the religion of our times, and its mode of worship is in the acquiring of ever increasing wealth, using whatever means it takes, no matter the consequences. Those in power are its priests and they deem that it's the duty of the rest of us to get jobs, work, make money, and hand it over as either taxes or in trade for trinkets. More and more people are beginning to become aware of this, and don't like being pressured into this mold. We commonly hear the problem described as "corporate greed," but anybody can be greedy: from the kindergarten bully who steals everybody's candy to the politician who takes bribes under the table. Some suggest that the answer to capitalism is socialism, but a government can be just as greedy, power hungry, fraudulent, self-serving, and uncaring as a big corporation. It's the human element that makes it so, and this is something no law can govern.

I think it is important that those of us who desire a self-sufficient lifestyle understand the underlying basis upon which we make decisions. How we assign value to things will influence those decisions and, I think, our ability to succeed as homesteaders. The problem is that a standard of value other than money is foreign thinking to us. It is not the mindset we are taught and it is difficult to think this way. Our challenge is to begin to look at ourselves and the things around us in a different light, because our sense of success will depend on how we evaluate our needs and how we expect to meet them. It will depend on where our sense of security lies. I do not believe that the consumer/profit mindset ultimately works for the homesteader. Not because homesteaders never buy or sell anything, but because the heart of the homesteading movement is about simplifying our lives, not about trying to replicate the modern 21st century lifestyle in a more natural setting. It's not that the homesteader is opposed to buying or selling, but that he or she is able to live without buying or selling if necessary.

As much as Dan and I strive for the agrarian mindset, I still find modern thinking creeping in. I often think first of buying something, rather than seeing if there is another way to meet that need, or evaluating if it is truly a need at all. As we've made repairs and upgrades on our old home, I catch myself wondering how much more we could sell the home for than what we paid. While some might say that is prudent, I have to remind myself that our house is our home, not an investment. We bought it to live in, not for its potential profit value. The difference is that it enables me to make decisions based on what I want and what meets our needs, not on what a real estate agent or potential buyers might think. There's a lot of freedom in that, and we're much happier with the end result.

This change in thinking is not easy. Still, I see the importance (for us anyway) of leaving the consumer/profit mindset behind if we want to make our dream come true. We need to learn to rethink our needs, rethink how to meet them, and rethink the true value of things. We need to learn how to be content with what we have. In the end, I think this will serve us very well.

NOTES

[1]Wendell Berry, *The Gift of Good Land: Further Essays Cultural and Agricultural* (San Francisco: North Point Press, 1981) 48.

CHAPTER II

DIFFICULT THINGS

Our two livestock guardian dogs, Kris and Kody. Kris, a Bernese Mountain Dog, died of autoimmune complications. Kody, a Great Pyrenees, was a chicken chaser. After getting caught with a dead chicken he was returned to his former owner.

There are almost too many joys to homesteading to name: first eggs, spring daffodils, chicken antics, baby goats, a productive garden, a pantry full of canned garden goods, eating one's first 100% homegrown meal, a feeling of independence and purpose, sensing the seasonal rhythm of creation. But there is another reality to it as well, and this is a hard one, filled with difficult things. These are the things we would like to prevent, to control, to fix; but that is the deception of human nature. Some things are beyond our ability to change, or are not meant to be controlled.

The animal pecking order is an example of this. As humans, we have the ability to be polite, to be respectful, to take turns, to share, to be fair. Animals do not have the least bit of consideration for these things, and can, in fact, be quite ruthless toward one another. Often the pecking order is established in blood, roosters will kill one another, and bigger animals will push the smaller and weaker ones out of the way. This is the way things are. The animals all know it and know their place. Humans are a non-factor and human intervention is temporary at best.

Death is perhaps the most difficult of the difficult things, although it is not exclusive to homesteading. Anyone who has ever owned a pet understands this. Since it is a primary function of pets to provide companionship, it is expected to allow oneself to develop a bond, an emotional attachment. In fact, we indulge in it. This makes it all the more difficult, even devastating, when the pet dies, disappears, or has to be put down. It's been that way with every pet we've ever had. We had one cat disappear, one die of feline lymphoma, and watched our puppy deteriorate before our eyes, in spite of our veterinarian's and our best efforts. My favorite little cat died of kidney failure due to the antibiotics she was given for enteritis. These are the kinds of things every pet owner has to face from time to time, and they are never easy.

Animals on the homestead bring a new dimension to this, especially if one chooses to raise animals for meat. Intellectually, at least, we understand the necessity of not getting emotionally attached. Some of the best homesteading advice I ever received was from a budding farmer. "Don't name the animals," she told me. Unfortunately, even when we're doing our best, baby animals do not all survive, predators will kill and maim, healthy looking animals sometimes drop dead for no apparent reason, accidents do happen, and disease does take its toll.

Dan and I decided, from the beginning, that all the animals on our homestead would be working animals. In exchange for being sheltered, fed, protected, and otherwise cared for, each would provide according to its natural function: cats for rodent control, guinea fowl for tick control, and a dog to guard. We have chickens for eggs, goats for milk, and both for manure and meat. On our part, we must provide them with a healthy, happy, safe environment. We also decided that being self-sufficient meant taking responsibility for everything we eat, including meat.

Our first farm animal experience was with chickens. When we ordered our chicks, we got straight run (i.e. mixed sex, theoretically 50/50). Our intention was to keep all the pullets (young hens) and one rooster. The rest of the roosters would be for meat. It was a deliberate decision and we understood that it was more than a mere intellectual one. Because of this, we tried to view our chickens in a certain light from the beginning, not as pets but as livestock. That's why we never named them. We had to keep in mind that their purpose was not to provide companionship, but eggs, meat, manure, and we hoped, more chickens. In addition, we had to view them with a sense of responsibility and stewardship, understanding that, someday, we will be accountable for how we have treated everything in our care.

Even so, the experience had its emotional ups and downs. The concept of killing a chicken seems straightforward enough, but we didn't know the step by step details of the process. We read the books and websites, only to discover that there are a number of techniques. This meant more decisions. Then there was the uncertainty of never having done it before, and the sense of clumsiness that comes with learning any new skill. Our sense of responsibility required that it be done quickly and with as little stress and suffering for the chicken as possible. Could we manage that the first time around?

A Welsummer hen with a mixed brood of home-hatched and mail order chicks. I slipped the hatchery chicks under her at night and she accepted them as her own.

In the end we bought a killing cone, and Dan slit its throat. We plucked it, eviscerated it, roasted it, and ate it. To be honest, it did not go as smoothly as we might have hoped and, the truth of the matter, at that point, was that we didn't know if we wanted to do it again. In spite of trying to steel ourselves against the emotion of the whole thing, we had the emotions of an awkward new experience to deal with anyway.

Still, we had 11 more young roosters in the chicken yard, some of which were becoming aggressive, greedy bullies. Local classifieds were filled with young roosters for sale, from folks looking for their own solution to the same problem. It made us re-evaluate. Our motivation to raise our own meat came not only from our goal for food self-sufficiency, but also from personal convictions about the sources of the food we eat. What were our other options? Take them to a processor? Well, that would take the "self" out of "self-sufficiency," wouldn't it? Give up eating meat?

In the end we pressed on. We allowed ourselves to experience the emotions of our inexperience, but did not dwell on them. We allowed ourselves time to learn and adjust to this new part of our lives. The rest of the processing went better, although I can't say we have this skill down to a science. Both of us will admit that it will never be our favorite thing to do, but like any other journey, the one to food self-sufficiency is taken one step at a time. Some steps are easy to take, others are not. The forks in the road must be thought out with care, and with a view to the consequences of the choices we make. Those who have grown up as farmers or ranchers have a better understanding of this. The farming mindset is more matter of fact because the death of animals is more a part of life than the rest of us are willing to admit. From the grocery store, we buy in neat, clean, sanitized packages what they have witnessed first hand.

Eating meat, of course, is a lifestyle choice, i.e. a choice of diet. Sometimes, though, difficult choices must be made for other reasons. Such was the case with our chickens two years later.

When we first ordered chickens, I chose four breeds: Ameraucana, Delaware, Barred Holland, and Welsummer. In my selection, I made sure that some of these breeds were known to go broody and be good mothers. It wasn't until the second summer that one hen, a Welsummer, finally decided she was ready to set on a nest. I gave her nine eggs, counted forward 21 days, and circled that date on the calendar.

I read that some folks have success increasing their flocks by introducing newly hatched chicks to a setting hen by slipping them under her at night. There were still a couple of other breeds Dan and I wanted to try, so this route seemed a good one to take. Introducing new chickens to an existing flock can have varying success rates, depending upon how willing the older chickens are to accept newcomers. This seemed a more natural way to introduce new chicks, and would hopefully be acceptable to the chickens. I ordered 15 Buff Orpington chicks, to be delivered as close to our expected hatch date as possible.

The baby chicks arrived two days before hatch day. When that expected day arrived, I kept a close eye on Mama Hen, watching and waiting. I could hear her clucking softly as she sat on her nest. A little while later, a tiny black chick head poked out from under her. Our first home hatched chick! She continued to encourage them and soon a second little black head emerged. That night I slipped the baby Buff Orpingtons into the nest, and waited anxiously to see how things would be the next morning.

I was greeted very early by a chorus of peeping. Mama was still on the nest, and the boldest chicks were already pecking away at the chick feeder. Once she was satisfied no more would hatch, she left the nest to tend to her new family. Of the nine original eggs, only two hatched out and one chick died trying. The other six eggs didn't hatch.

The next question on my mind was how well the existing flock would accept the new chicks. I'd heard stories ranging the gamut: from roosters helping to feed the baby newcomers, to roosters killing the whole lot, including the mama. I kept the chicks fenced off but visible, to give the established flock a chance to get used to the idea.

Our Barred Holland chickens. A white egg laying American heritage breed, ours were friendly towards us, but not towards the new chicks. It was war from the beginning.

When I started allowing the chicks to mingle with the adults, some of the hens would chase the chicks and in turn get chased by Mama Hen. Several of the hens challenged Mama Hen, but only once each. Apparently Mama had to reestablish her rank in the pecking order. Most of the older chickens gradually began to accept the newcomers, but two continued to be aggressive to the point of downright meanness. These were the two Barred Hollands, although I don't know if this is a breed trait or perhaps their individual personalities.

The hen, Lady Barred Holland, had been at the bottom of the original pecking order, and I could only assume that she was ensuring a new position for herself. Our rooster, Lord Barred Holland, was very territorial in regards to the hen house and chicken yard. Also he was very possessive of both his ladies and anything he thought they might like to eat. At times, he would chase the chicks relentlessly. Other times, he would completely ignore them. Any time he squawked, however, they would head for cover.

Only one thing made a difference. That was when migrating hawks began to frequent our fields. Lord B stepped up to the plate and even helped round up the chicks to protect them. We lost three hens to hawks during that time, but no chicks. After the hawks passed through, however, the line in the sand resumed as if nothing had permanently changed. The truce because of a common enemy had been only temporary.

As the young cockerels began to mature, Lord B was constantly crowing and chasing and cornering and attacking. We found one Buff Orpington dead, with its head stuck in the fence. Its neck was raw and bloody, and while I couldn't be sure, I suspected Lord B.

We really couldn't let the situation continue because Lord B was obviously not going to let up. One option would have been to process all the young cockerels earlier than we originally planned. That would eliminate the male competition, but His Lordship didn't like the pullets either. He was getting more ruthless in his chasing of them, all of them. The other option was to eliminate him.

This was tough to think about. He'd seemed a near perfect rooster: good personality, protective and deferential toward his hens, not aggressive toward humans, and provided us with hours of entertainment. He always came running when I called him, and would accompany us anytime we took a walk around the fields. No matter where we were outside, no matter what we were doing, he was always on the alert, always knew what was going on, always keeping an eye on us and the homestead. As he got older, however, he began to show more aggressive tendencies. He threatened to attack me twice for trying to shoo him, and Dan once, for imitating his rooster dance. This caused me to begin to keep an eye on him, but the real problem was that he was not receptive of the new chicks.

Eliminating him was not a choice we wanted to make, but something had to be done. In the decision making process, we had to set aside our feelings and fall back on our homestead goals. We would like to keep a

We're learning to make the best of difficult situations.

heritage, dual purpose breed flock. Initially we thought it would be Barred Hollands, because we really liked the look of ours. They and their eggs are somewhat small, however, so we considered other breeds. That was why we got the Buff Orpingtons. The bigger goal is to be as food self-sufficient as possible. That means we need to perpetuate our chickens. If Lord B wouldn't accept expansion of his flock now, then he wouldn't accept it next year either, or the year after that.

Lord B was the first rooster culled that year. Had circumstances been different, it was not the choice we would have made. It was his non-acceptance of the new chickens and the ongoing conflict and chaos which made it impossible to keep him. This dispatch went much more quickly and smoothly than the first time. Still, butchering chickens will never be something we'll actually like to do. Once the decision was made, we didn't dwell on it, we just did it. Emotions? A tinge of remorse beforehand; afterward, relief.

My hopes of, at least, a temporary peace in the chicken yard were short lived. As soon as Lord B was gone, somebody started crowing, almost nonstop. It turned out to be the cockerel His Lordship had picked on and chased the most. The entire flock sensed the change, and our original hens hung back that morning. The first to emerge from the coop was jumped on by about half a dozen of the cockerels. They chased her mercilessly and probably would have killed her if I hadn't intervened. Soon they spread out into the pasture, and the crowing competition commenced.

Things gradually settled down somewhat, but there were still squabbles and jockeying for new positions in the pecking order. Since the two groups of chickens never integrated into one flock, we essentially had two flocks who shared the same quarters. With their protector gone, my older hens were now the ones being picked on, especially those who had been meanest to the chicks. We later thought we should have done several of the cockerels at the same time, to upset their social order as well. That may have prevented some of the ganging up. This is something I would do differently should we ever be faced with a similar situation.

We eventually worked our way down to only one rooster. One thing we learned from all this is that having only one breed makes culling somewhat easier. They all look alike, so distinct personalities are obscure.

Two other things help. One is the advice to not think of them as pets, to make a deliberate choice to not develop an emotional bond to them. That's why we never technically named our chickens. Still, being new to chickens we couldn't help but spend a lot of time observing and admiring them, laughing at their antics, and giving one another chicken reports. Going into our third summer as chickeniers, we still liked having chickens very much, but the emotional novelty was finally gone. I think that's for the best and honestly don't know if there was any way to avoid it. Those who have homesteaded for at least several years will likely agree.

The other thing we learned is to not assign human emotions to them. They do have their own emotions, likes, and dislikes, but I have begun to realize that animals do not perceive life and death as people do. Humans place value judgments on life and death, and deem life the more valuable of the two. While animals have an instinct to survive, when death comes there is not the grieving and mourning amongst themselves as with humans. In general, there is acceptance and life goes on. This marks a distinct difference between us and them, which I personally think is specifically spiritual. Humans, after all, have spiritual decisions to make in life that animals do not.

Goats are another dual purpose animal we decided to raise, for both milk and meat. Although a family cow is often the animal of choice for these things, we didn't seriously consider a cow because neither Dan nor I

Some decisions are philosophically difficult, such as whether or not to disbud goat kids. Horns are beautiful and natural, but they can be dangerous for both the goat and others. Horns can be used for protection, but also to establish rank with other goats and humans. However, horns can get caught in fence, brush, or a cattle panel hay feeder (photo page 9), making the goat helpless against attacking dogs, coyotes, or other predators. Both male and female goats have horns.

can digest cows' milk. Plus, with our small acreage, goats seemed more feasible to keep and maintain. They are very versatile animals, and we could certainly use them for clearing our overgrowth of weeds and brush, something cows couldn't do.

While it was easy to agree on getting goats, it wasn't quite so easy to agree on a breed. I had kept Toggenburgs in the past, but favored getting Nubians because of their reputation for richer milk. Dan, on the other hand, liked the look of Alpines. Before making a decision, I researched goat breeds quite thoroughly. That was when I learned about Kinders.

The Kinder is a relatively new breed of goat, developed in the 1980s in Washington State. Kinder goats are mid-sized, dual purpose, and perfect for homesteaders. As a cross between Nubians and Pygmies, they inherit the very best of both breeds. To this cross the Pygmy contributes a number of qualities: smaller size, excellent feed conversion (high milk production on minimum food intake), heavier muscling (for better meat production), hardiness, aseasonal (year around) breeding, and multiple births (triplets and quads are common).

The Nubian genetics contribute longer legs (better for standing over the milking bucket), larger, easier to milk teats, a well attached udder, higher production of high protein, high butterfat milk, extended lactations (producing milk for as long as standard size goats), color, and the trademark "airplane" ears.

There are two ways to obtain Kinders: by either purchasing them or by purchasing a "Kinder Starter Kit". This consists of at least one registered Pygmy buck and one registered Nubian doe. Since there were no Kinders to be had within hundreds of miles, breeding our own seemed the only way to go. Toward that end we purchased two registered Nubian does and two registered Pygmy bucks.

Nubians are the most common dairy goat in our area, but it was not easy finding registered Pygmy bucks. The closest breeder I could find that first year was about 150 miles away, but did not have breeding age bucks for sale. Babies, yes, but considering the size difference between the Nubians and Pygmies, I figured too young a buck might not be able to fill such a tall order. That first year, I bred my does to a mixed breed dairy buck, and we enjoyed our first crop of baby goats, plus a bounty of rich Nubian milk.

Still, I kept my eyes open and eventually found a Pygmy goat breeder in the area. We purchased two bucks from him, one a mature four year old, the other a two month old buckling. Nubian breeding season is in the fall, so I figured we had at least one buck available, and a second for the following year. I wanted two of each breed to broaden my genetic base. That would give me a couple of years before we needed to worry about bringing in more goats.

We bought the bucks in late spring, after fencing off a pasture for them and building what we called Fort William, our buck barn. Made from our own logs in cabin fashion, it became a fine shelter for our billy boys.

My first set-back occurred several months later, when we lost our buckling. Even the vet was not sure what was wrong. There was no diarrhea, fever, loss of appetite, nor a heavy parasite load. One day the little guy was fine, and the next he was down. In spite of treatment, he was soon dead. This was difficult on multiple levels. It was emotionally difficult because we really liked him, but also it called to question my abilities as a goat keeper. I felt this was a failure on my part. On a practical level, it meant we lost much needed genetic diversity for our Kinder breeding program. At that point, however, there was little we could do but press on. With autumn approaching, we had another challenge to face.

That challenge, which is inherent in the Kinder Starter Kit, is the size difference between the proposed mating pair. Some Kinder breeders state the mission will be accomplished by the buck's desire and cleverness alone, while others use something like a straw bale to give the buck the height he requires. This is where we ran into difficulties. We didn't have any baled straw at the time, so once we figured out that our buck was too short to do the job without it, we tried leading a doe to a small ridge. If she would stand downhill with her rump facing the crest of the ridge, we figured he'd have a chance. We led the does to the correct position, but unfortunately our buck never quite seemed to catch on. Neither did the girls, who particularly did not like being made to stand in a specific spot.

Our next idea was to make a small platform. We placed one end on the crest of the ridge, and made it level with a couple of cinder blocks at the other end. We called it our "Pygmy buck assist." The idea was to place the doe in front of the platform with her back end up to it, and lead the buck onto the platform to do his job. Neither of our does was particularly

Our Pygmy buck assist

cooperative, however, and each in her turn refused to stand in front of it. Our buck, on the other hand, was willing, but seemed very insecure trying to attempt a mating from on top of the platform.

We were committed to this project, however, so in the hope that practice makes perfect, we continued with this method for several heat cycles. That the does continued to go into heat every three weeks was the indicator that neither had been bred. As the months passed and our does continued to go into heat like clockwork, I began to worry that there was a possibility our plan wasn't going to work. It was frustrating to deal with their apparent lack of cooperation. I finally threw up my hands, opened the gate between the buck and doe pastures, and said, "Fine, see if you can do any better by yourselves." I put the girls in with their husband and left them there for the next three months.

Once winter set in and breeding season was over, there was nothing left to do but wait. I marked my calendar with potential due dates, each 150 days after sighted attempts at mating, and prepared for the blessed events. Goat pregnancies can be determined by either ultrasounds or blood tests, of which I did neither. Girth size is not an indicator, not a reliable one anyway. A well fed goat will have a well developed rumen and can look pregnant when she is not. I just watched, waited, and hoped. Two months before the first due dates I dried my girls up. Expectant goats can be milked the first three months of their pregnancies, but need the last two for the growing kids.

Every due date came and went. In the end we were kidless, Kinderless, and milkless. It was a blow, but it was not the only one. The other one was Jasmine. Jasmine was one of my registered Nubian does. She was a large goat with a very sweet personality. She was a frustrating goat, however, because she always seemed to have something wrong with her. If something was going to happen, it would happen to Jasmine.

Jasmine had udder issues when I first bought her. The seller was upfront about it, and told me the problem had been resolved. At that time, only one half of her udder was producing milk. I naively accepted what the gentleman told me, that after she kidded again, the udder would be okay and resume functioning normally. At the time, that should have been a huge red flag and I never should have gone ahead with the purchase. But I did, and looking back I realize it was partly beginner's ignorance, and partly because she has good bloodlines. I thought I was following the sage advice to buy the best I could afford.

Shortly after I brought her home, she developed weeping sores on her udder. My vet verified that it was definitely infected and prescribed massive

My first two Nubian does, Surprise and Jasmine

doses of antibiotics. The bad news was that there was some necrosis of the tissue. He said this would slough off, but the teat would probably seal itself in the healing process. That meant she couldn't be milked on that side. He went so far as to suggest that if I was planning to cull any animals, she would be a candidate. Well, I was neither ready to cull her nor give up hope. I gave her the antibiotic and used an herbal salve on her udder. I managed to save the teat, but the question remained as to whether or not it was functional.

All of this happened the year before we got our Pygmy bucks, so at that time Jasmine had been bred to my Alpine cross buck. As her due date approached, I kept a close eye on her, and started putting her in the birthing stall at night. We had already had two successful kiddings and three healthy kids that year, so I had high hopes Jasmine's labor and delivery would go well too.

On the eve of her due date, I checked on her several times during the night. A little after 3:30 a.m., I discovered that she was in the second stage of labor. Everything seemed to be going normally at first, but after a while I began to worry that it was taking too long. I reviewed my books, and then went in to investigate what the problem was. It was a tail first presentation, which meant the best I could do was to try to find the hind legs and guide them feet first into the birth canal. This I was able to do, but even then, labor seemed to take forever. Her contractions were slowing down and she was exhausted. In the end, a little doeling was stillborn, likely due to compression of the umbilical cord, which cut off oxygen.

Jasmine was up and eating by daybreak, but never delivered the placenta. Also, her udder was very hard on the side she'd already had problems and I could not milk anything out. This time I drove no little distance to take her to a vet who was reputed to be an expert with ruminants. Not surprisingly, she had a uterine infection and mastitis. She was flushed out, given shots, and we went home with an armload of treatments and antibiotics.

At Jasmine's follow-up visit, she had more treatments and injections. Before we left, I asked the vet if she could be bred again. The vet told me she didn't see why not. Because of this, I decided I would keep Jasmine for another year and try to breed her to a Pygmy buck for Kinder kids.

During the following year Jasmine developed hoof rot. While I battled this, I began to wonder for the first time whether or not is was worth it to keep her. By then, we had our Pygmy buck, but for whatever reason, she wasn't cooperating with him. Her various problems during the two years I owned her had meant numerous trips to the vet and numerous hours of research. Add to that the cost of treatments and the time to prepare and give them, and she had taken a lot of time, money, and physical resources. While I never questioned my responsibility to do all this for her, I did begin to question something else.

The question I began to ponder was, does her contribution to the homestead and our goals balance out the constant parade of problems? This was not an easy question either to ask or answer, especially considering that we were still new to this lifestyle and did not have many goats, nor the means to replace the ones we lost. However, it was a make it or break it question in regards to our goal of self-sufficiency and I was, in fact, becoming exceedingly discouraged with all of Jasmine's health issues. Not just pity, but the constant need to treat her was tipping the scales; it was starting to take more time than I had to care for her. It was a question I had to ask and answer. My conclusion was that if she indeed kidded, I'd sell her and our wether (neutered male) as soon as her kid(s) were weaned. I confess I felt a mixture of both sadness and relief when I reached this decision. Still, if I could find a home for her with someone who had different goals and more time, I felt this would be the best course of action for both me and her.

Then the unexpected happened. Jasmine broke her leg. It was her shoulder actually. Neither Dan nor I witnessed it, but a few hours earlier there was a brief rain shower. Jasmine was out in the pasture at the time, and I saw her take off running toward the goat shed because goats hate rain. The most likely scenario is that she slipped and fell as she rounded the corner to get into the shed. When I found her, she was standing in one of the stalls with her left front leg dangling in an odd position.

Initially, we thought she'd dislocated it, but we were clueless about what to do. We called our vet in hopes we could treat this at home. She was a big girl (over 150 pounds), so getting her into the back of my jeep or Dan's pickup would be no easy feat. The vet said she would need to be examined in case of ligament damage, so we took her in. He could palpate a break, right under the shoulder, in a place impossible to splint.

Splinting a broken leg on a goat can usually be successful, but since this one couldn't be splinted, the conventional prognosis was not encouraging. Ordinarily, such an animal would be put down. Dan wasn't willing to accept that without more research, however. Also he wanted to verify whether or not she was pregnant. If she did have to be put down, we didn't want to kill the kid(s) too, if they had a chance to live. We had blood drawn for a pregnancy test and brought her home.

While we waited for the test results, I tried to make sure she remained comfortable, well fed, and had a clean stall and bedding. Several times a day I would go out and collect laundry baskets full of forage for her to eat. I also purchased purchased *Alternative Treatments for Ruminant Animals* by Paul Dettloff, D.V.M., and followed his recommendations for herbs.

The pregnancy test results were negative. I was disappointed on the one hand, but relieved on the other. As much as I had hoped for our first Kinder kids, I worried about labor, delivery, and active, nursing kids for Jasmine with her leg, or more likely, separating them from her and then bottle feeding them. However, it made the question of "earning her keep" all the more relevant, and more difficult. My initial decision to sell her with only half her udder functioning seemed unlikely enough. Now, depending upon how her leg healed, the problem was compounded, as was the decision about what to do with her.

In contemplating the options, there were a number of things I had to keep in mind. I had to remind myself that I cannot fix every problem, I cannot save every animal, and I must not take these as personal defeats. Nor do I want to fall into the trap of confusing responsibility with loyalty. This is not realistic for a self-sustaining homestead. Neither is focusing so much on only one animal, that everything else is neglected.

I continued to treat and care for Jasmine, still hoping her leg would miraculously heal properly. As time passed, it became apparent it wouldn't, and she had great difficulty getting round on only three. In fact, she finally gave up trying. We decided that the thing that made the most sense was to take her and our wether to a meat processor. It was not the way we had hoped things would turn out, but also we knew that real life is not always fair, nor "happily ever after".

While the situation with Jasmine was difficult, at least there was a definable problem, a broken leg. There was the lingering question of whether or not we could we have done something differently, but somehow knowing the cause and prognosis made it easier to accept. More difficult is illness that doesn't seem to respond to treatment, such as with our dog Kris, who died of complications from an auto-immune disorder.

My llama, Charlie, and our ever watchful rooster Lord B in the background.

The worst, however, is trying to deal with symptoms which do not define a specific problem or illness. Such was the case with Charlie.

When Dan and I first discussed protection for the goats, we talked about getting a livestock guardian dog (LGD). Then I found a llama breeder on Craigslist, who wanted to sell off her bumper crop of weanling llamas at a price we could afford. Even though a llama costs a little more than a dog up front, they are actually more economical to keep than dogs because their vaccinations are fewer and their diet simpler. In summer, they feed themselves on grass and browse, but even in the winter, they eat less hay than a cow or horse and require very little grain. As a handspinner, the added bonus for me would be the fiber. The name on his paperwork was Chocolate Drop, but I called him Charlie.

Llamas, by nature, are not like dogs, or cats, or even goats. Dogs, cats, and goats are friendly and affectionate. They love being petted and getting a good scratch. They make good pets. Llamas, on the other hand, are not pets, and they don't like being petted. They are companionable but not affectionate. They are inquisitive but aloof. They are curious but cautious. They are intelligent but like to keep their distance. Even mama llamas don't nuzzle and groom their babies like most other animals do their young. In spite of all that, llamas are very trainable.

Because of all this, I had to invest a lot of time in training Charlie. At the very least, llamas need to learn to be caught, haltered, lead, stand for shearing and hoof trimming, and load into a trailer. In addition, I wanted to train my llama for packing. The closest feed store wasn't that far away via the back way, and I could envision walking trips to buy grain or other livestock supplies.

During the five months that we had Charlie, Dan would comment on occasion that he didn't seem to be growing. I reassured him that llamas are slow to develop and wasn't concerned until he seemed to be losing weight. Twice he had diarrhea, for which fecals indicated parasites, so he was treated for these, and given probiotics and an electrolyte/vitamin supplement because of the diarrhea. These problems could have interfered with weight gain, but even when everything was normal, he continued to lose weight.

I talked with other llama owners on a llama forum about feed and weight loss, and switched from the sweet feed recommended by his breeder to a llama formulation. When that didn't help, I started offering it to him twice a day. I continued to give him probiotics and made sure he had a good free choice mineral supplement. I offered treats of carrots and apples, but he really wasn't interested in these. He continued to get thinner.

As the days went by, he grew weaker, although he was still eating and his beans (droppings) were normal. I started taking him out to fresher grazing in the yard, worrying because he was having trouble getting up and seemed wobbly on his legs. I had to force him to get up and move, because somehow he seemed to stop caring. It was at that point that I began to wonder if llamas could have such a thing as Failure To Thrive (FTT). I started to research, and discovered that it is actually quite common with young llamas. The causes of it are extensive and too often, by the time FTT is identified, it is too late.

His last morning, he couldn't lift his head up. I had already accepted that he was dying, but his death was no less devastating to me. When it finally came, I was flooded with grief, as well as a sense of a burden having been lifted. Dan was on the road at the time, but we spoke by phone and agreed on a burial place in the woods.

For Charlie, my best guess is that he was was weaned too young. He was advertised with a group of weanling llamas, described as being approximately 5 months old. Llama experts don't recommend weaning before 6 months of age, which means his digestive system probably hadn't developed enough to obtain the nourishment he needed from grass, hay, and grains alone. He still needed his mother's milk. He was hungry and eating, but his body was not capable of absorbing the much needed nutrients. The probiotics weren't enough to make a difference.

Even though I did everything I knew to do, Charlie's death was one of the hardest and it was difficult not to take as a personal defeat. As humans, we want to control the circumstances in our lives. We want to control the outcome of the situations we are in, and when they don't turn out, we demand to know reasons why. We are quicker to blame than to accept. In reality, nature is neither compassionate nor kind. Nor does it place greater value on life than on death. This is difficult for those of us in the modernized 21st century to understand. We don't have enough experiential knowledge of the natural world to understand its processes and how we fit into them. We do not understand that some things are beyond our ability to control, and that these things require only acceptance on our part. We do not know how to cope with things that a less industrialized culture accepts with grace.

The only way to avoid experiencing animal death is to not keep animals. For Dan and me, however, the human/animal relationship is an integral part of the agrarian way of life. One can become vegan, and grow only vegetables, fruits, legumes, and grains, but difficult decisions will still

I still miss Charlie.

still come. Mice and rats will come to eat the grain. Then snakes will come to eat the mice and rats. We can grow more grain to support the growing rodent and snake populations, while we try to pick mouse poop out of the wheat. This might be a viable choice for some.

Some homesteaders try to maintain animals in a no-kill environment. I respect this choice but don't envy them another problem. Eventually an animal will be so sick, or so severely injured, that it would be cruel to allow it to continue to suffer, such as our situation with Jasmine. If one has monetary wealth there might be veterinary solutions to prolong life to make ourselves feel better. If one is trying to be self-sustaining, a certain amount of vetting is necessary and desirable, but as with all things, decisions must still be made.

Of all the things faced by the aspiring homesteader, I think these are the most difficult with which to deal, the most difficult to learn to accept. Our struggle points back to the problem of mindset, and how far from natural reality our sophisticated culture has become. While Dan and I strive to learn the physical skills necessary to homestead, we have discovered that there are emotional skills to learn as well. Acceptance without blame is one of them.

CHAPTER 12

WORK SMARTER, NOT HARDER

"Never stand up when you can sit down. Never sit down when you can lie down." Attributed to Winston Churchill, Kris and Kody demonstrate the principal.

This is a chapter I'm writing with a little less confidence. So far, I've shared what we've experienced and what we've learned. This chapter, on the other hand, is about something we are just beginning to figure out. You might say this chapter is still being written. The concept of working smarter, not harder, is one that we are realizing is vital to our success at homesteading. Perhaps, if we had a large family living at home and plenty of helping hands, we might not even think of it. But we are a family of two, old enough to have grown children out on their own, and experienced enough to realize that the strength and vitality of youth will not last forever. We are realizing that we must learn to ration our time and energy. We cannot afford wild bursts of enthusiasm which lead us down rabbit trails. Nor do we need to start projects that will increase our work load in the long run. There are things we need to accomplish if we are working toward self-sufficiency, but we need to do so intelligently, and without running around like chickens with our heads cut off.

Long before we bought our homestead, I homeschooled my kids. When I first started, I set about creating a classroom. I did it because this was the concept I was familiar with when I thought of school and education. True, I'd have less students (just two), but I thought I needed a particular room with desks, a blackboard, a bulletin board, a globe, a dictionary, a computer, and bookshelves for school books, workbooks, and supplies. It didn't take long to figure out that these things have nothing to do with teaching and learning.

It was similar when we started our homestead. We had certain ideas about gardening, farming, and livestock, ideas about how things are supposed to be done. While these were heavily influenced by books such as Laura Ingalls Wilder's *Little House on The Prairie* series and Ralph Moody's *Little Britches* books, they were still rooted in a more modern concept of farming. Farms look a certain way, crops are grown a certain way, and the various tasks associated with farming require the right equipment. One grows crops and manages animals according to established customs, and one doesn't, say, plow a half acre of ground with a garden tiller.

If we'd had the money, we probably would have run out and bought all the equipment and accouterments associated with farming: tractor, plows, fencing, livestock, hay baler, log splitter, and materials to build a "proper" barn. We fretted about this somewhat in the beginning, and not having these things has meant we've accomplished less than we might have liked. Having limited funds, however, has turned out to be a blessing in disguise. True, we've had to do a lot more by hand, ending many a day with aching muscles reminding us that we're not getting any younger. On the other hand, it's forced us to begin to think outside the box.

Realizing there are other ways to do things started with my goats. As far as I knew, kids were separated from their mothers at birth and bottle fed. There are several rationales for this. One is knowing how much milk the kids are getting. More importantly, it is preventative for a disease called caprine arthritis encephalitis (CAE). This incurable goat disease is passed on through the mother's milk. Precautionary measures include removing the kids immediately after birth and bottle feeding either pasteurized milk or a milk replacer. Although this is only necessary if the mother is infected, it was considered standard practice for a long time.

Lily, one of my Nubian does with her Nubian/Kiko cross (Kikobian) twins.

Somewhere along the line, folks started wanting a more natural way of keeping goats. I learned about it when my two of my does were pregnant, and I was researching labor and delivery for goats. I learned that kids do not have to be pulled from mothers who are CAE negative. Those with "clean" herds often let the kids nurse directly from their dams. To make both kid rearing and milking easier, it is possible to pen the kids near their mothers at night, milk the mothers in the morning, and let the kids nurse them for the remainder of the day. I was delighted to learn all this. It's better for the goats and would ease my workload as well.

My next breakthrough came with my chickens, when I learned about the deep litter method for the chicken coop. Conventionally, chicken coops are cleaned out weekly, as needed, or not at all, which gives them their reputation for an offensive odor. The deep litter method approaches coop keeping with the same concept as composting. The litter is kept truly deep, starting with six inches and adding more as needed. If it begins to smell, there is too much nitrogen and not enough carbon. The key to successful deep litter is the availability of lots of carbonaceous materials such as chopped straw, dried grass clippings, dead leaves, etc. By "lots," I mean a ratio of something like 30 parts carbon to 1 part nitrogen[1]. By

A variety of non-compacting materials can be used as chicken litter. I like leaves and grass clippings. If it begins to smell, more litter needs to be added. If I scatter a handful of scratch in the coop every day, the chickens keep the litter stirred up.

continually mixing these materials into the litter, there is no unpleasant smell. Instead, the chickens have thick, warm bedding, which gives them hours of entertainment as they scratch around for bits of grain or bugs to eat. The material breaks down and pre-composts, and I only have to clean out the coop a couple times a year. I get the benefit of less work and plenty of material for sheet composting in autumn, or adding to the compost pile.

The garden is another area in which we're learning "work smarter, not harder" strategies. When we started gardening a couple decades ago, it was customary to till or plow the entire garden every year. By the time we started a garden on our new homestead, many gardeners had switched to permanent raised bed, no-till gardening. We realized that for the vegetable garden, at least, this would save quite a bit of labor. We did not make the beds raised because of cost, but we did mark out permanent beds and terrace the garden with downed logs from the property. There are several benefits with permanent beds. One is that we are able to improve the soil only where it needs it. There's no sense composting ground that will become garden walkways. Also, because the pathways are permanent, compacting the soil along them is not an issue. And if the weeds are kept under control with heavy mulch, there is no need to routinely till the soil.

Another garden concept I've expanded on is companion planting. The theory here is that some plants grow and produce better when in the company of other, specific "companions." I had used this somewhat in the past, and then read *Great Garden Companions: A Companion-Planting System for a Beautiful, Chemical-Free Vegetable Garden* by Sally Jean Cunningham. She uses companion group planting. This utilizes the same polycultural approach as permaculture, but focuses more on annual fruits and vegetables. Rather than planting only two compatible plants together, the idea is to plant whole beds with a large variety of companion plants. This includes vegetables, flowers, and herbs together in the same bed to create those companion groups. One of my most successful examples is a combination of tomatoes, sweet peppers, marigolds, borage, and sweet basil. The beds are so full that there are less weeds, the soil stays moist longer in dry weather, and everything thrives. Once the plant groupings are worked out, it is simple to rotate the groups to different beds every year.

Companion group beds. Front: Sunflowers, summer squash, and marigolds Next: Okra, egg plants, habanero hot peppers, and cosmos. Behind: Sweet potatoes, dill, and summer savory. Topmost bed: broom corn, marigolds, and cucumbers.

Simplifying our diet has helped too. Every summer I've experimented with things I used to buy from the grocery store, but have never grown myself. My experiments are great when something new does well. If it does poorly or takes too much fussing, I'm realizing that we probably don't really need it. What I do need is to adapt our diet to what we can grow. It makes more sense to concentrate on things that grow well here, rather than trying maintain special growing conditions for things that don't.

A related concept is to rely more on seasonal foods. This means we not only eat fresher foods, but also, at least in my part of the country, I need to preserve less. Because of our mild winters, I can harvest root crops all winter long if I mulch them well. Between that and a longer growing season, working smarter means less freezing, dehydrating, and canning, especially of vegetables. Besides having more fresh eating and less work in preserving, it leaves more room in my freezer, another plus because I need the space for meat, eggs, and things like blueberries, which don't can well and we don't care for dehydrated.

For some foods, such as canned soups, pizza sauce, and jams, I save the work until a less busy time in the season. I do this by freezing fruits and whole tomatoes. If fact, it's far easier to peel thawing tomatoes than the traditional boiling water and ice water dunks. The tomato peels slip off easily when the frozen tomato is thawed slightly in a bowl of lukewarm water. Jams and jellies are just as good from frozen fruit, and my canned soups may contain previously frozen ingredients such as tomatoes, okra, and meat. For me, this is a work smarter method for food preservation. I avoid feeling rushed to get the harvest preserved, plus I enjoy canning more when the temperature isn't summery hot.

Another area I'm trying to work smarter in, is seed saving. Seed savers face the challenge of cross-pollination, so care must be taken to preserve pure seed. Different types of corn can be managed by staggering plantings, so that my field corn, sweet corn, and popcorn aren't pollinating at the same time. Some plants flower all summer long, melons for example. I find these more difficult to deal with because they will cross-pollinate too. I reasoned that seed saving would be less work if I grow cantaloupes one year and watermelons the next. We have less variety per season, but we enjoy variety over the years.

Another major "work smarter, not harder" breakthrough came the second summer we grew field corn. The first summer had been a learning experience, and there were certain problems I wanted to avoid the second go-round. Well, one big problem - weeds. Corn production was pretty fair that first year, but the weeds were out of control. We don't have a farm

Work smarter strategies for food preservation. Top: Using an onion bag for blanching squash for freezing. Bottom: Freezing tomatoes for easy peeling, just dunk in warm water.

Rows of corn "weeded" with a lawn mower. I found that the weeds acted as a ground cover and helped keep the soil from drying out during hot, dry weather. Of course, I'm only able to do this because I deal with small, quarter acre plots.

tractor with which to cultivate, and we refused to use chemical herbicides, so weeds were a huge problem. Because a quarter of an acre of corn is a lot to weed with a hand hoe, Dan used the tiller to do some weeding at first. Of course the weeds grew right back and by the end of the summer, I couldn't get to the corn plants. Heck, I couldn't even see some of them for all the morning glory vines. When I lamented about this on my blog, a reader mentioned using a lawn mower for the same problem. Thanks to her suggestion, I was able to clear a path and harvest my corn.

When we prepared for our second summer of growing field corn, I wanted to include this in my planting plan. We divided the field into two sections, one for corn and the other for cowpeas. When I marked my rows for corn, I measured the width of my lawn mower and planted accordingly.

When Dan got ready to till for the cowpeas, it occurred to me that perhaps we didn't need to till the entire plot. If I was going to mow between the rows anyway, why not just till where I was going to plant the seed? As expected, the weeds came, but by mowing between the rows, I could at least get to the plants. What I didn't count on, was how long the cowpea runners would grow. These intertwined across the rows, making it more difficult to mow after the plants matured. Still, the plan helped.

The following summer I refined my strategy even more. I planted double rows of corn, each double row a lawnmower width apart. When the corn was five or six inches tall, I planted cowpeas in the double rows too. This allowed the cowpeas to use the corn as bean poles, and benefited the corn with the nitrogen fixing cowpeas.

My lawnmower became my tool of choice, once again, when our soil remineralization project was delayed, as detailed in chapter 7. By the time I tracked down where to order the soil amendments, it was too late to plant. Hot dry weather is not the time to be planting pasture. Even if the seeds sprouted, the roots would likely burn up in our hot dry summer weather. We decided to wait until fall to plant.

It is said that nature abhors a vacuum, and that certainly is the case with bare soil. Having made the decision to wait on planting the pasture, the area we had cleared was free to grow whatever. And it did. I knew I couldn't stop it and that the goats and chickens would still benefit. My concern was that all the unwanteds growing there would go to seed and perpetuate the very problem we were trying to eliminate.

That was the first time it occurred to me to use the bagging attachment that came with our lawn mower. Until then, I couldn't see the point of a bagger. In fact, until it became a weed control tool, I couldn't see the point of a lawn mower, except to knock the flowers and seed heads off the weeds in the front yard. My longterm goal for the front yard is permaculture landscaping, so that we will have no lawn to worry about. In the meantime, why bother to bag up the clippings just to make the lawn look prettier. The neighbors should be glad it gets cut at all. But when my future pasture was loaded with growing weeds that I didn't want reseeding, it occurred to me that I could actually bag and use those clippings elsewhere. And use them I did: for chicken litter, goat bedding, compost, compost worm bedding, and to cover muddy areas around the goat shed.

Hand mowing a half acre field and emptying the bag frequently is still a lot of work. The point, however, is not in having no work, but in having the work manageable and productive, not overwhelming and with no other purpose than cosmetic. The point is to work smarter, not harder.

Two books that helped greatly in this regard are *Sepp Holzer's Permaculture* and Joel Salatin's *You Can Farm: The Entrepreneur's Guide to Start and Succeed in a Farming Enterprise.* We began to see how we could partner with animals for mutual benefit. Keeping livestock in permanent pens or paddocks might be traditional, but it is not the most

Trellises and tomato cages used to be a headache. Now, removable cattle panels tied to permanent t-posts are used for vining plants and for tying up tomato plants.

effective way, and, in fact, creates its own problems. The potential for overcrowding lends itself to disease and to offensive odors from the buildup of urine and manure. Why not just let animals do what they were designed to do? Goats can clear unwanted brush, pigs can turn soil while hunting for things to eat, chickens can clean up parasites while they spread manure and eat weed seeds, turkeys can help with weed control, and guinea fowl eat ticks and other insects.

After our first field corn harvest, we turned the goats and chickens into the myriad of weeds that had grown with the corn. The result was that our goats, in particular, were healthier looking than on pasture alone, and all our critters were happier.

This started us thinking about how we could implement a comprehensive plan to feed not only us and our animals, but the land as well. In our original master planning, we'd chosen specific areas for animals, pasture and forage, and for crops. The half acre we'd designated as a grain field had been neglected for many years before we bought the place. The weeds I'd been battling, particularly vining plants such as blackberry, kudzu, and morning glories, were well established there. We spent two summers fighting these, plus what seemed like hundreds of other weeds, as well as sapling trees. One day Dan suggested that perhaps this field was a better place for pigs than crops. Instead of struggling to nurture plants there, why not let pigs have at it? Pigs root things out of the soil to eat, acting as natural tillers. We'd read of others who used this to their advantage, why couldn't we? It made more sense to grow field crops in another area, where the battle to find them wouldn't be as difficult.

Crop rotation is not a new concept, but with Dan's idea, I began to think about it in a more comprehensive way. Why just rotate field crops within a designated grain field? Why not rotate them with forage, hay, and animals? Do we really need our fields designated for one purpose only: one for crops, one for pasture, one for hay, and one for pigs? No pasture remains perfect and all pasture areas eventually require maintenance, because weeds will always come in and eventually take over. In permaculture, this is called succession. For us, with goats that thrive on many of those non-pasture plants, why not take advantage of it?

If we can learn how to rotate animals, crops, and pasture, we can hopefully develop a cycle. This won't be a no-till scheme; it will be a natural till alternative. We realize it won't produce a neat, tidy, manicured looking farm, but it seems a better plan for stewarding our homestead.

How well this plan will work, I do not know at this time. It is an example, though, of trying to think through our needs and problems, and trying to find solutions that work with nature, rather than against it. It's trying to work within the parameters of the way things are, and learning to utilize what's available to us. Likely, changes will need to be made along the way, as unforeseen problems present themselves. Evaluating our success will take years. Slow living is slow because it is seasonal living. What we do know is that the conventional methods of managing land and livestock will not work for us. To be truly sustainable, it is vital to manage the land in a way that improves it over the years, rather than depletes it.

As you can see, much of what we've learned in regards to working smarter, not harder, is experience based, with a lot of nonconventional thinking as well as trial and error. Because not all of our ideas work well, it is a challenge not to see problems and set-backs as failures. Slow progress can, at times, be discouraging. We sometimes look around us and see only the things needing to be done, not what we've already accomplished.

Working smarter, not harder, is knowing what the priorities are and learning how to discern the relative importance of the choices at hand. For us, the primary goal is working toward self-reliance. The projects we choose must conform to that goal. Under that, we have prioritized areas of importance. The animals and food come before upgrading the house. That's not to say that structural repairs are neglected. The roof for example, had to be replaced in a timely manner to avoid water damage from rain. On the other hand, I wouldn't be surprised if there are folks who drive by our house, notice it's need of paint and repair, and wonder why we don't do something about it. We are doing something about it, in accordance with our priorities. Proper housing to meet our animals' needs is more important than the aesthetic appearance of our own house.

A sense of pressure to accomplish tasks may come from outside influences, or from within. The opinions of others is one example of an outside influence, weather is another. Sometimes it's a race against time to get soil tilled and planted before a rainstorm hits. We have little control over this. What we can somewhat control is the pressure we create for ourselves by our own expectations. Setting time frames for projects, for example. We're learning that our assumptions of how long a job will take may not be realistic. This has been especially true of repairs on the house. We might think it will only take half a day to replace a window, until we pull down the siding and discover extensive water damage and wood rot underneath. Many a day has ended with the frustration of only accomplishing half of what we set out to do.

Another challenge is pacing ourselves. At our age, the need for this is evident physically. Sadly, our energy levels and physical abilities begin to wane as we get older. This, in turn, can lead to that sense of urgency to get everything done, everything accomplished. I sometimes ask myself, what if we don't get it all done? What if we never reach our goal? What if we never attain energy independence, pay off the mortgage, or get the woods fenced? These questions put me at a mental crossroads of sorts. The choices before me are frustration and discouragement, or acceptance. This is not the acceptance of defeat, this is acceptance with grace. We've all heard the phrase about taking time to smell the roses. To be able to live the life of our dreams without enjoying it, is little better than never living it.

To many folks, farming or homesteading is a lifestyle they would never consider because it's a lot of work. Well, that's true, but the idea of making a living by doing nothing or simply having fun is neither realistic for most of us, nor healthy for any of us. Working smarter, not harder, means productive work, not busy work. It means time and priority management. And, especially, it means feeling good about what we do.

NOTES
[1]Joel Salatin, *You Can Farm* (Swope, VA: Polyface, Inc., 1998) 285.

CHAPTER 13

WHERE DO WE GO FROM HERE?

As Riley ponders what's next, so do we.

In previous chapters I talked about the challenges we have faced as we work toward fulfilling our dream of self-sufficiency. In some areas, I think we have made good progress, such as growing and preserving much of our own food, even some of our animals' food. And we have learned a lot through both research and experience. Still, we have a way to go. Once a year, we set aside some time to look back over our goals, plans, problems, and progress. We take a look at our master plan, evaluate what we've accomplished, discuss changes that ought to be made, and decide what we think needs to be done next. Because it's so easy to lose long-term perspective in day to day living, our annual evaluation enables us to step back and focus on the big picture once again. As we evaluate our projects, we also evaluate our priorities. Each year, we make a goal list of what we hope to accomplish next.

My early dreams were of garden and orchard overflowing with produce, and a pantry stocked with every every fruit and vegetable imaginable, bins of grain, containers of herbs, pickles, jams, jellies, jars of homestead honey from our own bees, and homemade apple cider vinegar from our own apple trees. These dreams have not changed but, rather, have been adapted. We've learned that some things don't grow well in our part of the world, not everything grows equally well every year, and some things are very time consuming and labor intensive to keep on hand. On top of all that is the weather. Weather is food growing's biggest challenge. Some years it's horrific heat and drought. Other years it's endless cloudy days and flooding rains. Neither extreme makes for good gardening.

All of this points to the often unspoken uncertainties of working toward a self-sustaining food supply. There simply are no guarantees, which is probably why folks were so willing to leave the farm when the industrial revolution swept through.

I have come to realize that, for this endeavor to be successful, there are some things that I need to rethink. I need to relearn concepts I have about food and eating if I'm going to consider our lifestyle a success. I come from a grocery store background, where variety and picture-perfect produce are the norms. The time of year doesn't matter; everything is always available and always beautiful.

I've had to rethink our diet. While it is certainly possible to grow everything we like to eat, it isn't realistic. Perhaps, if all we had was the garden, I could do it, but our life is more than just the garden. It makes more sense to simplify our diet. This is the nitty-gritty of local and seasonal eating. We eat what we have and we preserve or store the extra. This means learning to live with less variety ("What? Eggs again?") as well as many non-traditional meals ("Vegetable soup for breakfast?)

I've had to rethink quality. It's interesting to read books such as Barbara Kingsolver's *Animal, Vegetable, Miracle*, or *Growing A Farmer* by Kurt Timmermeister, because these point out that grocery store standards are not the norm in the natural world. In the real world, foods taste different (usually better) and look different (usually worse). I've had to discard my standard of perfection. Nothing is thrown away simply because of a bad spot or a few bird pecks. Just cut that off and feed it to somebody else; chickens, goats, and pigs are only too happy for such tidbits.

I've had to rethink my expectations. I can't "count on" anything. For example, the year goat breeding was a failure and none of our does had kids. That meant no milk, cream, butter, cheese, yogurt, kefir, or ice cream. One rainy summer our blueberries and figs produced bumper crops, but

Relying more on winter gardening means needing to preserve and store less.

the garden did not. Some things were a no-show such as peppers and egg plants. Other things produced, but not in huge quantities: cucumbers, tomatoes, and okra. Even my nine laying hens only gave me two or three eggs per day that summer. I can say it was likely due to too much rain and too little sun, but my plans of bulging my pantry shelves with pizza sauce and pickled okra dissolved into wondering how we'd make it without pizza every Friday night.

I've had to rethink food habits. This is actually a tough one because we get used to preparing and eating certain foods. Sometimes it's the convenience of grabbing a box out of the cupboard and simply adding water. Sometimes it's because these foods comfort us, our personal "soul" foods, the foods we grew up with (like macaroni and cheese made with Velveeta.) These are the foods we tend to crave.

The biggest challenge is learning to be content with our lives, just as they are right now. Learning not to be dissatisfied with what we have, learning not to fret when abundance isn't there, learning not to worry about what the future will bring. I've heard it said that worrying is like paying interest on a debt one doesn't owe. Who wants to do that?

Most things in the self-sufficient lifestyle, even when I'm doing my best, are beyond my control: weather, germination rate, or animal deaths. Ultimately, it makes no sense to worry about them. Yet human nature likes

Unplanned but necessary projects sometimes present themselves, such fencimg the blueberry bush to protect it from the goats. They would love to eat it to the ground.

things predictable and wants a guarantee on every outcome. But God's natural world isn't that way; the point being, I think, so that we learn not to rely too much on ourselves. True contentment implies trust.

Dissatisfaction, often disguised as ambition, is what keeps us unhappy. We assume contentment means complacency because we humans want to make our mark upon the world! That may be a virtue in worldly society, but for the homesteader it is a liability. Yes, we need to be realistic about our goals and how we plan to achieve them, but we need to balance that with thankfulness for what we've already accomplished.

I wish I could say I've mastered all this, but I can't. I can say that these are things I am working on learning, new habits I am cultivating. I see them as being key in our quest for self-sufficiency, and truly, for all of life.

On the practical plane, there are areas we need to develop and improve. Grains and other field crops are examples. For these, we need to master threshing and winnowing grains such as wheat and oats. Honey and sorghum syrup for sweeteners are other examples. All of these reflect the need for specific equipment and skills. We also need better areas for curing, processing, and storing bulk items such as grains and beans. In addition, we will continue soil improvement in all areas: the garden, orchard, fields, and pastures. We will continue remineralizing our soil, focusing on one area each year. Even so, feeding ourselves and our animals will always be a challenge because it is dependent upon many of those factors beyond our control.

Planting, harvesting, breeding, and kidding are examples of ongoing things; things for which a seasonal routine must be developed. That routine is the basis for the agrarian way of life we long for. Other things are a part of that, too, such as pasture maintenance, because pasture and forage areas do not maintain themselves. I envision a four or five year rotation amongst these as a part of our ongoing homestead routine.

Many other projects are one time projects, necessary for establishing our homestead but, once accomplished, free us to move on to other things. Fencing, planting fruit trees, animal shelters, rainwater catchment, a greywater system, and, especially, repairs to our house are examples. As we gradually check these projects off the list, we see our homestead taking shape. As one time projects, they will still require maintenance in the future, but unless some disaster hits, such as a tornado, a barn, for example, only needs to be built once.

Our house, in the neighborhood of 90 years old, came with many structural problems: threadbare roof, leaky chimney, sagging floors, rotting siding, water damage under windows and around the toilet, cracked window panes, outdated wiring, and scanty insulation. As we've addressed these, we've tried to do so with our long term goals in mind, such as plumbing repairs with a view to future greywater recycling. The repairs and changes we make to the house enable us to utilize our living space in a manner that facilitates our lifestyle: woodstove alcove, wood cookstove, summer kitchen, and larger pantry, for example.

Current house repairs and upgrades are focused on the bedrooms and hall bathroom. Besides the plumbing problems in the bathroom that need to be addressed, these northwest facing rooms receive frigid blasts of wind during winter, and the baking setting sun in summer. With proper insulation, energy efficient windows, and summer shade, we hope to reduce our energy needs as we make much needed repairs.

While we are beginning to make progress on our water conservation plans, farther down the road is energy self-sufficiency. Although neither solar nor wind power seem feasible for us, we can still focus on smaller projects such as a solar water heater. We can explore other avenues, such as biogas to at least power the refrigerator and freezer, or perhaps a wood-gas powered generator and battery bank. Much research is still needed, but these are projects we contemplate for the future.

Work on the house is more than cosmetic. In the bathroom a sheet of vinyl flooring hid a rotting floor, water damaged from the leaking toilet. We have also installed an energy efficient window, insulation, and paneling. A before photo is on page 12.

For the animals, our current focus is housing. Even though we've been able to modify and make do with our existing outbuildings, they, like our house, are old. We have made modifications and repairs as needed, but some measures, such as tarping a leaking roof, are only temporary at best. As we've developed a routine with our animals, we have contemplated a better set-up, one that will meet both their needs and ours for dairying, kidding, brooding, pasture rotation, storage for grain and hay, etc. After housing, we plan to continue fencing the property, especially our wooded areas. This will provide not only forage, but will keep invading kudzu at bay (goats love kudzu). We recently added guinea fowl to the homestead, and have plans to eventually add turkeys, pigs, and honeybees.

There are other things on our master plan for which we have no agenda yet, the pond and greenhouse for example. They have low rank as priorities and whether or not that changes, remains to be seen. By being part of the plan, however, they still shape our bigger picture. This is important as we determine which projects are next.

Of my goal to breed and raise Kinder goats, much discussion and deliberation has taken place. When it looked as though our second breeding season was going to be as unsuccessful as our first, I decided other things were more important than focusing on a specific breed. I loved the idea of dual purpose goats for both milk and meat but, unfortunately, my Pygmy/Nubian combo wasn't working out. Surprise, my remaining Nubian doe, had been through three heat cycles that second year, with no sign of settling (getting pregnant in goat folk talk). I could not justify letting her go another year without kids and, as much as I loved the idea of Kinders, it was time to reevaluate the goal. The bottom line was, how do Kinders fit into our primary goal of working toward self-sufficiency? We want goats for brush control, milk, meat, manure, and something to trade or sell. Other types of goats could do that too.

About that same time, Dan had been admiring a meat breed of goat known as the Kiko. I found a Kiko breeder in the area and bought a large, ten month old buck. Surprise liked him immediately. Mating was successful and five months later she gave birth to a buckling. As a Kiko/Nubian cross, I laughingly tell folks he is my first "Kikobian." I don't know if such a cross will produce a true dual purpose breed goat like the Kinder, but I'm hoping it will produce goats that are less high maintenance than the Nubian while still giving high yield, good quality milk, and like the Kiko, gain weight well on available forage without a high grain diet.

Of all these plans and projects, I can only say that if we had been younger when we started our homestead journey, we probably would have approached it more methodically. We would have focused on the house first and then added a large garden, orchard, fencing, barn, livestock, grain field, and the ability to make our own electricity. We figure we don't have enough years to do it that way, so we have approached all these things on simultaneous fronts. We keep a house project and an outdoor project on the front burner at all times, with unplanned projects, maintenance chores, and routine work to round it out. This can be frustrating, however, because we always feel that we have a lot of loose ends.

As the big, one time projects are completed, we look forward to a time when our lives will no longer be dictated by the next self-sufficiency project on the list. We look forward to developing a seasonal routine, one based on the rhythms of spring, summer, fall, and winter. That seasonal lifestyle, which is a hopefully simpler lifestyle, is one of the reasons we were drawn to the homesteading life in the first place.

Part of that simpler lifestyle will mean less trips to the store as we rely more on growing, gathering, and doing for ourselves. Directly, that's a savings on time, fuel, and wear and tear on the car, but indirectly it means less trips to the recycling center and landfill. Perhaps I've been a bit slow to figure this out, but one day, while we were getting ready to make a trip to dispose of recyclables and trash, it occurred to me that the only things we throw away come from items we purchased, not from what we produce on the homestead. While we waste nothing that we grow, gather, produce, or raise for ourselves, our trash bags were filled with wrapping, packaging, containers, broken parts, and broken items, all from things we bought. On top of that, I am required to buy plastic trash bags in order to throw the stuff away. Even if I'm able to recycle most of it, I need containers and space to store it all, plus it takes time and fuel to remove it from the property, either my time and fuel, or a city's service (with the additional cost of paying for that service).

This chore of life is something most of us probably take for granted, but it is frustrating on many levels. As a conscientious inhabitant of the earth, it goes against my sense of responsible stewardship to throw anything away. As a consumer, it's frustrating to know I've paid for every scrap of packaging and filler I have no use for, because those costs are passed on to the consumer. As a homesteader it can be downright discouraging, because it means I'm still far too dependent on the consumer system. Worse, it is completely contradictory to my goals of self-reliance.

Industry's answer to this is recycling. Many products and packaging are now manufactured with recycled materials. Unfortunately, these often come with a higher price tag. I suppose the rationale is that consumers will willingly want to pay more for the sake of saving the planet. In my way of thinking, if manufacturers are really wanting to do something to help the environment, shouldn't these cost less, to encourage folks to buy them?

The eye opener for me was when we lived in Florida. I was researching starting an herb farm, and somehow got a free subscription to a small business owners magazine. The first issue was about businesses going green. This was right up my alley, so I read it from cover to cover. When I set the magazine down, I was dismayed. Not one article, column, tip, ad, or letter to the editor ever once mentioned environmental concerns, responsibilities, or motivations. The entire gist of the magazine was about profit, and concerns about decreased profits because "green" products are more expensive to manufacture. The advice focused on advertising tips, semantics, gimmicks, how to balance the cost with short cuts, and using environmentally friendly products to bait customers.

The more I contemplate a self-reliant life, the more I realize that our 21st century lifestyle, with all its choices and conveniences, comes with a price. That price comes in the form of overflowing landfills and pollution from the byproducts of the manufacturing process. Recycling is one good answer, assuming the recycling process is more energy efficient than the manufacturing process, which isn't always the case. Even so, recycling is only a new innovation because trash and garbage are a relatively new problem. Before the industrial age, folks had less. In having to make do with less, they were creative and clever with what they had. They produced very little actual waste. This was their way of life. This is the way of life I want as well.

Unfortunately, our economic system is now based on manufacturing rather than agriculture, and on ever increasing profits and consumer spending, rather than meeting needs. Consequently, we have become trapped in a buy/waste cycle, so that the only way to truly waste less, is to buy less. However, we are repeatedly told that confident consumer spending is the key to economic health and growth, the key to jobs, the key to pulling us out of the recession. When we stop purchasing, companies lay

Above: a compost worm bed. We try to waste nothing. Food scraps that cannot be fed to the animals are fed to the composting worms. The castings go into the garden.

folks off, jobs become scarce, and we approach economic disaster. So, more buying = more waste = destroy the planet; less buying = less waste = economic disaster. What a conundrum!

Such realizations demand action, and I'm no exception. Rather than jump on some bandwagon, however, it makes more sense to approach this on a personal level. It makes more sense to rethink our own lifestyle, not only what we buy, but what we eat, how we use water and electricity, etc. My ultimate goal is a no waste way of life, and for Dan and me, this is an important motivator toward self-sufficiency. It's a lifestyle choice, one that some might think severe. For us, it's what we should have been doing all along. It is what we are working toward now.

Another lifestyle choice that we entertain is the question of whether or not it's possible to make a living from our land. This seemingly simple question is rather complex to answer. On the surface, it seems to be asking if can we become career farmers. Or, if not farming, can we establish some sort of homestead based business, such as selling herbs, farmstead cheese, or handcrafted items?

On a more basic level, the question which must be asked and answered first is, what does it mean to make a living? $30,000 a year? $90,000? $150,000? More? Less? Obviously there is no one size fits all answer. The monetary needs of a young family of two adults and three children is vastly different from an empty nest family of two middle-aged adults. But does that income include supporting three pets, two vehicles, a $250,000 mortgage, cable TV, and internet service? How many cell phones? Does it include insurance, college savings, and retirement investments? Does it include credit card payments and other debt? Does it include building a new barn, installing an off-grid electrical system, and buying feed for the livestock? Will making that living require two incomes? Or can it be managed on one? How we answer these questions sets the framework for everything we do in regards to homesteading. We must determine our expectations in terms of required income, which means we must decide the kind of lifestyle we want to live.

Dan and I have always lived more frugally than most. Except for our mortgage, we've stayed out of debt. When we've needed something, we've saved up the money first, then purchased it. We've made do on one income, and that a modest one. That's meant doing without many things typical to the modern American lifestyle: cable or satellite TV, new vehicles, new fashions, going out to eat, dry cleaning, air conditioning, convenience foods, and until recently, a cell phone for Dan because he's out on the road. Because of that, however, we've learned to be content with less. At this point in time, we have basic bills to pay: mortgage, utilities, mandatory insurance, basic phone and internet services, and property taxes.

As we increase our self-reliance in specific areas, food and energy for example, our monetary needs decrease; my electric bill goes down and I no longer need to spend as much at the grocery store. By not going to the grocery store as often, my fuel costs go down and I save wear and tear and maintenance costs on my vehicle. For now, the money we save in these areas is put back into establishing our homestead. Eventually, once established, we won't need as much income. The goal is to reduce our financial needs so that, perhaps, we truly can make our living from our land.

In the past, we have tried to make a go of the handcrafts business, Dan with his pyrography and me with my handspinning, handweaving, and knitting. Neither of us was successful enough as to be particularly encouraging. I've considered, too, that if we really could make a go at these, they would be so time consuming as to leave little of the day for the many homesteading chores we do. Most folks seem to end up putting more hours into a home business than they do a regular "9 to 5" job. Self-sufficiency on the other hand, is a full time job in itself.

Now that we have our five acres, we have more recently been contemplating making a living at farming. We have read two well-known works on this topic: *Five Acres and Independence: A Handbook for Small Farm Management* by Maurice G. Kains, and *You Can Farm: The Entrepreneur's Guide to Start and Succeed in a Farming Enterprise* by Joel Salatin. It was the first book that motivated us (Dan especially), toward the homesteading life we are living now.

While both of these books might be categorized under the same topic, there is an interesting contrast between them that is worth noting. *Five Acres and Independence* was first published in 1935, long before the term permaculture had been coined. It was written when the future hope of farming was in science, and before government regulations, food industry standards, and insurance companies began to dictate much of what a farmer could and couldn't do. It includes use of chemical fertilizers and other industry based improvements, which promised to bring the subsistence farmer more than a life of just getting by. Seventy-five years later, Joel Salatin writes after the fact. *You Can Farm* focuses on common sense and working with natural processes, rather than trying to conform to a scientific system. It is this thinking outside the conventional box that Dan and I have discovered to be vital to our sense of success.

Making a living from the homestead is a topic we entertain frequently. My weaving studio, formerly the sun room (page 12), is currently used for storage as we make repairs and upgrades on the house. After that, I hope to get back to weaving.

But does that mean we can make a living at it? That question is still unanswered. At the time of this writing, Dan continues to work as a over-the-road truck driver. He chose a company for which he is out for three or four days at a time, and then has 2 or 3 days home to work on projects. It pays less than being on the road for weeks at a time, but we have enough to pay our bills and pay as we go on improvement projects. It is frustrating for him, however, because having to go to work means slower going on projects at home.

Ideally, our goal is that eventually, after we establish our homestead with all its big, one-time costs, we will in reality need very little cash. That by the time we reach "retirement" age, we will have implemented lifestyle changes and become self-reliant enough to minimize our need for cash. The goal is that we'll only need enough money for the necessities we can't provide for ourselves. The question is whether or not we'll be able to recognize when we get to that point. The challenge is that as our expenses decrease, can we think of it as needing less money? Or will we think of it as having more money to spend? It is so easy to think of things on which to spend money. There is always another project, another improvement, something else that might be useful, something else that appeals. But when is enough, enough? Learning how to make do and be content with what we have is an ongoing challenge.

We had the opportunity to test this not too long ago; to test how well prepared we actually are to live without money. The situation was unexpected, which made it all the more real. It was brought about because of our desire to be debt-free.

Our mortgage is our only debt and while we are able to pay down on the principal, the realities of Dan's job make this a slow process. The trade-off, as I mentioned before, is having more time at home to do things that need to be done on the homestead. We've talked, from time to time, about his going really "over the road," as in long haul driving where he'd be out three weeks at a time, and home for two or three days. This is not our preferred lifestyle, but we've wondered if it would be worth it for several years if it meant being able to own our place free and clear.

One day on a whim, he applied to a flatbed and heavy haul company based in Texas. It would mean little home time, but it would double his salary. If we were willing to make sacrifices, we truly had the potential to get our mortgage payed off, we hoped within a few years. They hired him within days and flew him to the main office in Fort Worth for orientation. He was then assigned a truck and was on the road in a week.

His second week out he developed severe pain in his leg and ankle. He could neither walk nor shift the big truck gears. The home office wanted him to go to the emergency room, but stipulated he had to sign a form taking full responsibility to pay for it. Well, Dan didn't want to go to the emergency room. They insisted and he finally agreed to do it, but would only sign the form if he added "as required by my employer." They balked at that and the matter was turned over to workers comp.

Since he was out on the road and couldn't drive, it took them a day or two to get him back to the home office. He was immediately called in to see the big boss, and let go. He was told he was rude to folks (who weren't available to corroborate) and that he wasn't a good fit for the company.

That was shocking enough, but the more immediate problem was that they fired him 1000 miles away from home. It wasn't just getting Dan home, but also all his gear. An over-the-road driver's truck is his "home away from home." Truck stop prices are exorbitantly high, so most truckers have a plug-in cooler or fridge, 12 volt cooker, water container, bedding, cooking and eating utensils, tool box, first aid kit, CB radio, etc. plus enough food, personal supplies, and clothing to last their trip out. The company offered to buy Dan an airline ticket and later ship his belongings home. Considering their handling of the situation as well as the attitude of the boss, Dan was unwilling to go this route. He wanted to take everything with him. Next, they offered to reimburse him for renting a vehicle to get home. With that option we were faced with paying for it upfront which would, for the most part, wipe out our bank account.

Initially we thought we would be okay, because he had made quite a bit of money in those few weeks with the company. When he tried to rent a vehicle from Texas to home, however, he could get neither credit nor debit approval for the amount. He gave me a call and I went online to check our bank account, because I knew we had more than enough money to cover it. I was quite shocked to discover that the trucking company had stopped payment on his first paycheck, to revoke his sign-on bonus and orientation pay. We later learned that legally they can do this during the 90 day probationary period for new drivers.

We had just enough in our savings account to cover it. I transferred it to the checking account and we were able to get him home. Fortunately, his old company was willing to hire him back. The bad news was that it would take two weeks to formalize the hiring paperwork, plus another two weeks before the first paycheck would arrive. Having drained our savings account to get him home, we were left with only $500 on which to live for the next month. It was time to take a hard look at how well prepared we were for an emergency.

Emergencies can take on many forms. Many believe that our economy and culture are in a precarious state and are preparing for the worst. While Dan and I agree with this assessment, we have never considered ourselves preppers, doomers, or survivalists. It has made more sense to begin to disengage ourselves from the materialistic way of life that our current system fosters. Working toward at least some degree of self-reliance has made more sense to us than simply stocking up on supplies, or taking measures to keep our wealth secure. A hoard of gold isn't going to mean much if there is no food to buy.

More realistic are other types of emergencies such as weather events, accidents, illness or, as in our case, an unexpected job loss. Fortunately, the bills had been recently paid so that was not a worry. Because we had focused first on food self-sufficiency, we ate very well during those four weeks without having to buy a thing. Because I am a stock-up shopper, we had a good supply of the basic necessities such as salt and toilet paper.

We were fortunate because we knew our situation was temporary. We knew how long it would last. Still, it made us take a hard look at ourselves and our lifestyle. The biggest concern was being able to make mortgage payments. But also, I realized that life is considerably simpler when one doesn't have any money. There were no worries about how to spend our money wisely, because there wasn't any to spend.

Some might say, but how can you live without money? What if you get cancer or are in a terrible car accident? To that I can only say that I refuse to live my life based on what-ifs. I refuse to live in fear of what may or may not happen. If the worst does happen, we will meet it as we do all challenges, to the best of our ability.

We live in uncertain times. Our economic system and hence our culture, as they are now, are not sustainable. Our country, indeed our world, cannot live with eternally increasing debt any more than a family can. Eventually there are consequences. People point to a number of causative factors, such as corporate greed or our dependence on oil. They look to government for solutions, fiercely debating political strategies for correcting the problems. True, our tax dollars have supported solar electric companies and put up a few more windmills, but other than for politicians to brag about at campaign time, how has it helped the ordinary folk? I don't see that it has. Nor will it unless someone is willing to make the alternatives affordable for the average citizen, or at least pass on the savings to the consumer. It's true that sacrifices will have to be made to correct the problems, but I often wonder why they can't be made by someone other than the little guys on the bottom rung?

I admit Dan and I often question how far we'll get in our quest for self-sufficiency. There just doesn't seem to be enough time and, ironically, enough money to achieve our goal. The temptation is to become discouraged, to think of success as having a list of self-sufficiency boxes all checked off. The challenge is to not think of it as a race against time, but simply the way we live. We can either fret over what we haven't accomplished, or we can take it one day at a time, experiencing whatever that day has to offer, and making our progress one step at a time. It is that less complicated, hands-on lifestyle that drew us to homesteading in the first place. We are learning that that, in itself, can be enough.

Where do we go from here? We simply continue our journey, our quest toward self-sufficiency. We try not to view bumps in the road as set-backs, but simply take them in stride. If life presents detours, we make course corrections as needed. Most of all, we try to enjoy our life and be thankful. I know for me, there is no other way I want to live.

DOING WHAT WE OUGHT

"Everybody's not going to do that."

I have been confronted with this statement several times over the years, always in a conversation about my lifestyle, often as an interruption from a disinterested bystander. Besides being a conversation stopper, this, of course, is a true statement. So obviously true, that I admit I find the interjection odd, especially because I never initiate such a conversation in the first place. I consider my lifestyle a personal matter and, as such, have no interest in actively promoting homesteading. However, I am always happy to answer questions or share experiences with someone with similar interests. In a real life context, I simply bite my tongue and politely agree, though I confess I'm usually thinking, "Then why did you ask," or "I wasn't speaking to you in the first place."

Some readers of this book may be thinking the same thing, that everyone is not going to do what Dan and I are doing, pursuing a life of self-sufficiency. I would say that some folks won't see the point at all, but then, they would likely never pick up this book in the first place. Some might be curious in general, or have selected similar interests: gardening, permaculture landscaping, backyard chickens, home food preservation, cooking from scratch, remodeling an old house, simpler living, goats, water conservation systems, alternative energy, spending time outdoors, etc, although in a different context. Not everyone is going to want to try to put it all together in a self-reliant lifestyle.

Other readers may be interested in pursuing the same thing, the lifestyle that has come to be known as homesteading. To those, I hope our experiences have been of interest and perhaps even helpful. Unfortunately, there is no cookie cutter formula to successful homesteading. Our regions, properties, climates, food preferences, needs, inclinations, finances, and circumstances are important parts of the equation, but different for each of us. Likely, you cannot replicate what we're doing here, any more than we can do exactly what someone else is doing. Still, it would be my wish to encourage you. To let you know that there are ups and downs, joys and struggles, and that there are others attempting the same journey.

One thing I have realized, however, is that in spite of our different interests and lifestyles, most folks recognize that there are problems in the world. While we may not agree on the solutions, I believe we would all agree on the goal, that the world ought to be a kinder, gentler, safer place. I do not believe, however, that the best laws in the world can make it so. I believe that, in the end, it will all boil down to how each one of us chooses to live our individual lives. I believe that if each one of us would simply begin to live the way we ought, the world could not help but become a better place for everyone.

We ought to be kind to one another. We ought to be polite. We ought to share and take turns. We ought to be willing to help. We ought to respect one another. We ought to clean up after ourselves. We ought not to demand of others what we refuse to give ourselves.

We ought to take responsibility for ourselves and participate in the process of caring for ourselves. We ought not to expect others to do for us what we can do for ourselves, nor take from them when we already have enough. We ought not be lazy, ought to have a good work ethic. We ought to be accountable for our actions. We ought to leave things better than how we found them. We ought to make a positive impact on our environment, our communities, and one another. We ought to be moderate in consuming and with our resources. We ought to be considerate of the needs of others, and not take or use more than we need.

We ought to give ourselves permission to learn and make mistakes. We ought to be able to admit when we're wrong, and be able to back track or change direction without feeling like we've failed.

We ought not to ridicule others for their mistakes. We ought to give them a chance and the space to learn and grow too. We ought not to personalize the things that others say, but treat them with the same respect and tolerance we expect they should extend toward us. We ought not to be threatened by the opinions, beliefs, politics, religion, and lifestyles of others. We ought not to look for personal validation by expecting folks to think, feel, and live as we do.

We ought to be doing these things because they are the right things to do. Many of you reading this book will probably agree. This is how we ought to be. We can also agree that not everyone will choose to live as they ought. And there's the rub. If every person chose to live as they ought, I believe most, if not all, the world's problems would not exist. And, as right as it seems, we cannot force it upon others. Human nature is naturally independent, likes to make its own decisions, and does not like to be told what to do. Many good laws fail because of this. Laws attempt to govern behavior, but cannot govern attitude. Ultimately, it is an individual choice. My hope and my prayer, is that you will choose wisely.

HOMESTEAD RECIPES

A SAMPLING OF RECIPES WELL SUITED TO
HOMESTEAD RAISED INGREDIENTS.

The lid to my recipe box. The box was a Christmas gift from my husband and woodburned by him. See the entire box at http://danspyroart.blogspot.com/.

Green Bean Broccoli Salad
& "World Famous" Croutons

Okay, the croutons are not truly world famous, except in our little homestead world. I find they are a good way to use up stale or leftover bread and a tasty addition to any soup or salad. This salad is a nice way to use leftover canned green beans. The black olives and dressing are both non-homestead treats.

Green Bean Broccoli Salad (adjust proportions as desired)

green beans, canned or leftover cooked
broccoli, fresh picked, chopped
tomato, chopped ripe
black olives
olive oil
balsamic vinegar

Toss all ingredients together and top with croutons. Dan likes his sprinkled with grated Parmesan cheese.

World Famous Croutons

Cut bread into bite-size pieces. Toss with melted butter or olive oil and seasonings of choice (salt, pepper, herbs, garlic powder, Parmesan cheese, etc.). Spread out on baking sheet and bake until golden brown.

Recipe Notes:

I put odds and ends of bread into the freezer until I need another batch of croutons.

Instead of heating the oven to bake only croutons, I often time the making of them to go into the oven after I've turned it off from another baking project. The leftover heat browns them nicely. I just have to remember to remove them before I preheat the oven for something else. (Another lesson learned the hard way.)

STUFFED SUMMER SQUASH

This is an excellent summertime entrée, and a perfect use for any overgrown summer squash, including zucchini. A vegan version would be even easier to make, simply sauté your choice of vegetables for the filling.

INGREDIENTS:

1 overgrown summer squash
1/2 pound bulk sausage
small onion, chopped
2 slices homemade whole wheat bread, cubed or in crumbs
grated cheese of your choice , ricotta, or cottage cheese
salt & pepper to taste
grated Parmesan cheese

TO PREPARE:

Cut squash in half lengthwise. Bake or steam until it begins to soften. In the meantime, pan cook the sausage with onions. When the squash is cool enough to handle, scoop out the insides to make little boats. Add the scoopings, bread crumbs, grated cheese, and seasoning to the sausage. Mix well and spoon the mixture into the squash boats. Sprinkle with Parmesan cheese and bake at 350° F /180° C until golden brown, about 20 to 30 minutes.

Recipe Notes:

Another very adaptable recipe, simply substitute whatever meat, non-meat, vegetables, cheese, and seasonings you wish. Try leftover steamed brown rice instead of bread crumbs.

I've never done well growing regular globe type onions, so my onions are multiplier onions which grow well for me. They don't grow as large as globe varieties but are just as tasty.

Goatherd's Pie

Here is a tummy warming winter entrée. This is my homestead version of Shepherd's Pie, using 100% homegrown ingredients, including the goat meat. Technically labeled chevon from the French for "goat," it is called cabrito in many parts of the U.S. This hearty casserole is quick to make from leftovers.

Ingredients:

Cooked chunks of chevon, about 2 cups (can use home canned)
Leftover cooked vegetables, about a cup
1 pint condensed tomato soup, (yummy home canned)
A couple cups of leftover mashed potatoes (or can make fresh)
Butter, melted (of course I use goat butter)

To Prepare:

Mix meat, veggies, and undiluted tomato soup. Season as desired and pour into a 2 quart casserole dish. Top with mashed potatoes and drizzle with melted butter. Bake at 350° F /180° C, uncovered, until casserole is bubbling and potatoes are golden brown, about 30 minutes or so.

Recipe Notes:

Of course you can substitute ground meat for the chunks, or any meat for the chevon. Also you can replace the tomato soup with leftover gravy or broth. My mother always made Shepherd's pie with tomato soup, so that's what I think of with fond memories.

If your family likes turnips (or you just want a no-carb alternative), you can mash and substitute mashed turnips for the mashed potatoes.

CRACKLIN' CORNBREAD

Cracklins (cracklings) are the bits of unmelted fat and meat leftover from the process of rendering animal fat (see page 65). They are highly prized for flavoring.

Preheat oven to 425° F /220° C. Heat a 10 inch cast iron skillet containing:

  1/4 C lard, bacon grease, or oil (I used my rendered goat fat)

Mix together dry ingredients:

  1 1/2 C cornmeal (homegrown, homeground)
  1/2 C all purpose flour (adjust these proportions as desired)
  1 tsp baking soda
  1 tsp salt

Mix together wet ingredients:

  1 large egg, lightly beaten (my Ameraucanas lay my largest)
  2 C buttermilk (if no buttermilk, I use whey)

Stir together dry and wet and fold in

  1 C cracklings (I like mine finely chopped)

Pour batter into piping hot skillet. Bake until golden brown and an inserted butter knife comes out clean, about 25 minutes. Serve hot.

Recipe Notes:

Fat - You can use whatever fat or oil that suits your fancy. Some recipes call for adding the melted fat to the batter; I pour the batter directly into the hot fat in the pan. The result is a delightfully crispy cornbread.

Leavening - Many (most) cornbread recipes call for both baking soda and baking powder. Baking powder contains baking soda (the base), cream of tartar (the acid) and a corn starch buffer to slow down their reaction to one another. It's the chemical reaction between the base and acid that causes the batter to rise. The baking soda and buttermilk or whey have the same chemical reaction, so that the batter will rise without baking powder.

SWEET POTATO HONEY PIE

This was originally a pumpkin pie recipe that I adapted for sweet potatoes. I like it better than pumpkin. A bonus – this recipe is dairy free.

CRUST:

    1 1/3 cups flour
    ½ tsp sea salt
    ½ C lard (I use our rendered goat fat)
    1 egg plus cold water to = ¼ C (or enough to get desired consistency)

Preheat oven to 425° F /220° C. Cut lard into flour and salt mixture. Beat egg into water and add to flour mixture. Mix with a fork (not hands) until moist. Roll out and place in pie pan.

FILLING:

    2 C sweet potato, mashed or pureed
    3/4 C honey
    3 eggs, beaten
    1 tsp cinnamon
    1/4 tsp cloves
    1/4 tsp allspice
    1/2 tsp sea salt

Mix sweet potato, honey, & eggs. Add remaining ingredients and blend well. Pour into unbaked pie shell. Bake for 10 minutes at 425° F /220° C then decrease to 350° F /180° C and bake another 30 minutes or until an inserted knife comes out clean. Cool. May serve with whipped cream.

Recipe Notes:

The type of fat you use in the crust will make a difference in flavor.

Rendered animal fat, such as lard, makes the flakiest crusts.

Canned Green Tomatoes for Frying

When autumn's killing frost arrives, many a gardener is left wondering what to do with their abundance of green tomatoes. Recipes for these abound, but I love to can the largest ones for frying; a tasty winter treat.

To Can:

    Green, unripe tomatoes, medium to large in size
    Canning salt
    Citric acid or lemon juice
    Boiling water

Slice tomatoes, about ½ inch thick. Pack into sterile, wide mouth quart canning jars. Add ½ teaspoon salt and ½ teaspoon citric acid or 2 tablespoons of lemon juice per quart. Fill jars with boiling water leaving 1/2 inch headspace. Adjust lids. Process in boiling water bath for 7 minutes.

To Fry:

    Green tomato slices, drained
    Flour, seasoned with salt and pepper to taste
    Cornmeal, homegrown, home ground
    Egg, beaten with a little milk
    Fat or oil of your choice for frying

Coat tomato slices with seasoned flour. Dip slice in beaten egg mixture and coat in cornmeal. Pan fry until golden brown in about 1/4 inch fat. The tomatoes were precooked during canning, so this doesn't take long.

Recipe Notes:

Citric acid or lemon juice is necessary to lower the pH of the tomatoes to make them safe for boiling water bath canning. I find that citric acid (which I keep on hand for mozzarella making) adds no flavor.

Bread crumbs may be substituted for the cornmeal or flour. If preferred, you can use either flour or cornmeal for both coats.

Sauerkraut

Lacto-fermenting is something I had not tried until we bought our homestead. I first learned about it in a book entitled, <u>Preserving Food Without Freezing or Canning: Traditional Techniques Using Salt, Oil, Sugar, Alcohol, Vinegar, Drying, Cold Storage, and Lactic Fermentation</u>. My recipe is a combination of one of its recipes with one from Sally Fallon's <u>Nourishing Traditions</u>.

Ingredients per quart:

Shredded cabbage (a large head yields about 3 quarts)
1 tablespoon sea salt
¼ cup whey (if available, optional)
juniper berries (about 10 per quart)
hot, non-chlorinated water

To prepare:

Scald wide mouth canning jars and lids
Pack shredded cabbage tightly in jars, adding juniper berries as you go.
Add salt and whey
Fill jar with hot water to the brim
Seal with lids leaving no air space

!!! IMPORTANT !!!

Check contents daily. There are two reasons for this:

1. The fermentation process is anaerobic so the cabbage must be completely submerged in the liquid or it will grow mold.
2. During fermentation pressure builds up, so the jars must be opened daily to release it. Crocks do not have air-tight lids, so if using a crock, this would not be a problem.

Let the jars sit at room temperature for three days, then store in a cool, dark place. I refrigerate mine because our summers offer no cool places. The directions say it's ready in about a month's time, but you can taste it at any time and eat it when you like. The longer it sits, the more sour it will become.

Recipe Notes:

Salt inhibits the growth of putrefying bacteria until enough lactic acid has been produced to do the job itself. The addition of whey is not necessary, but speeds the process because it is a source of lactic acid.

Chlorine inhibits the lactobacilli, which produce the lactic acid. If only municipal, chlorinated water is available, the chlorine can be boiled out or allowed to sit for 24 hours to evaporate the chlorine. (I learned that trick when I used to keep tropical fish.)

An alternative method to covering tightly is to weight the contents to submerge them in the brine. This is a little tricky with quart jars, but can be done. Just keep checking to make sure no mold is forming on floating contents. If it does, discard the moldy part. The rest of is still good to go.

Individual jars are convenient for small quantities, but sauerkraut can also be made in any non-metal container, such as a crock. When I do that, I measure the water, salt, and whey by the quart, adding until I cover the contents of the crock. I weight with a saucer and pint jar filled with water, and cover the whole thing with a dish towel to keep the contents clean.

Lacto-fermenting is not limited to cabbage! The same method can be used for any vegetable or combination of vegetables.

As mentioned, the product continues to sour with time. If you find a particular sourness that you and your family prefer, it is possible to can your sauerkraut at that time. The downside to this is that the heat from canning will destroy the friendly bacteria and enzymes. Because of that I've never tried this and so not know the details of that process.

APPENDICES

RESOURCES

Listed here is my bibliography as well as additional information for the books and products I mentioned. I'm not necessarily endorsing these, just giving you a starting point for your own research. The bibliography for Appendix C is separate, and listed there.

BOOKS

Bellenger, Jerry, *Raising Dairy Goats the Modern Way*. Pownal, VT: Storey Communications Inc, 1994.

Berry, Wendell, *The Gift of Good Land: Further Essays Cultural and Agricultural*. San Francisco, North Point Press, 1981.

Colby, Pat, *Natural Goat Care*. Austin, TX: Acres U.S.A., 2001.

Cooper, Jane, *Wood Stove Cookery: At Home on the Range*. Pownal, VT: Storey Books, 1977.

Cunningham, Sally Jean, *Great Garden Companions: A Companion Planting System for a Beautiful, Chemical-Free Vegetable Garden*. Emmaus, PA: Rodale Press Inc., 1998.

Detloff, Paul, *Alternative Treatments for Ruminant Animals*. Austin, TX Acres U.S.A., 2009.

Emery, Carla, *The Encyclopedia of Country Living: An Old Fashioned Recipe Book*. 9th ed. Seattle: Sasquatch Books, 1998.

Fallon, Sally with Mary G. Enig, Ph.D., *Nourishing Traditions: The Cookbook that Challenges Politically Correct Nutrition and the Diet Dictocrats*. Washington D.C.: New Trends Publishing, 2001.

Gardeners & Farmers of Terre Vivante, *Preserving Food Without Freezing or Canning: Traditional Techniques Using Salt, Oil, Sugar, Alcohol, Vinegar, Drying, Cold Storage, and Lactic Fermentation*. White River Junction, VT: Chelsea Green Publishing Co., 1999.

Holzer, Sepp, *Sepp Holzer's Permaculture: A Practical Guide to Small-Scale, Integrative Farming and Gardening*. White River Junction, VT: Chelsea Green Publishing, 2011.

Kains, Maurice G., *Five Acres and Independence*. New York: Dover Publications, 1973.

Kinsey, Neal, *Hands-On Agronomy: Understanding Soil Fertility & Fertilizer Use*. Austin, TX: Acres U.S.A., 2009.

Kingsolver, Barbara, Animal, Vegetable, Miracle: A Year of Food Life. N.p.: Harper Collins, 2007

Logsdon, Gene, *Small-Scale Grain Raising,* White River Junction, VT: Chelsea Green Publishing, 2009

Ludwig, Art, *Create an Oasis with Greywater.* Santa Barbara, CA: Oasis Designs, 2009.

--- *Water Storage: Tanks, Cisterns, Aquifers, and Ponds.* Santa Barbara, CA: Oasis Designs, 2011.

Mercia, Leonard S., *Raising Poultry The Modern Way.* Pownal, VT: Storey Books, 1990.

Moody, Ralph, *Little Britches: Father and I Were Ranchers.* Lincoln and London: University of Nebraska Press. 1991

Pitzer, Sara, *Homegrown Whole Grains*, N.p.: Storey Publishing, 2009

Raymond, Dick, *Garden Way's Joy of Gardening.* Troy, NY: Garden Way Inc. 1982.

Rombauer, Irma S. and Becker, Marion Rombauer, *Joy Of Cooking,* Indianapolis: Bobbs-Merrill Co. Inc. 1980

Salatin, Joel, *You Can Farm: The Entrepreneur's Guide To Start and Succeed in a Farming Enterprise.* N.p.: Polyface, Inc., 1998.

Sloane, Eric, *A Reverence for Wood,* Mineola, NY: Dover Publications, Inc. 2004

--- *Diary of an Early American Boy,* Mineola, NY: Dover Publications, Inc. 2004

--- *The Seasons of America Past,* Mineola, NY: Dover Publications, Inc. 2005

Watt, S.B, and Wood, W.E., *Hand Dug Wells and Their Construction,* Warwickshire, UK: Practical Action Publishing, Ltd.

Wilder, Laura Ingalls, *Little House on the Prairie.* N.p.: Harper Collins, 1991.

WEBSITES

5 Acres and A Dream. 04 May 2009 Weblog. 10 Sept. 2013 <http://5acresandadream.com/>.

Acres USA. Publishers. Web. 10 Sept. 2013 <www.acresusa.com>.

Berkey Water Filters. Web. 10 Sept. 2013 <http://www.berkeyfilters.com/>

Bomgaars Web. 10 Sept. 2013 <http://bomgaars.com>.

Build A Solar Cooker (solar cooker plans). 10 Sept. 2013 <http://solarcooking.org/plans/>.

Build It Solar The Renewable Energy Site For Do-It-Yourselfers. Web.10 Sept. 2013. <http://www.builditsolar.com/index.htm>.

Cooperative Extension System Offices, USDA. Web. 10 Sept. 2013 <http://www.csrees.usda.gov/Extension/>.

Country Living Grain Mill, Web. 10 Sept. 2013 <http://countrylivinggrainmills.com/>.

Craigslist Web. 10 Sept. 2013.<http://www.craigslist.org>.

Daniel Tate Pyrographic Art. Weblog. 10 Sept. 2013 (recipe box) <http://danspyroart.blogspot.com/2013/01/large-recipe-box.html>.

Easy Digging (Italian Grape Hoe), Web., 10 Sept. 2013 <http://www.easydigging.com/>.

Excalibur Food Dehydrator, Web. 10 Sept. 2013 <http://www.excaliburdehydrator.com/>.

Heartland Appliances, (Sweetheart Wood Cookstove) Web. 10 Sept. 2013. <http://www.heartlandapp.com/>.

Hobby Farms, Web. 10 Sept. 2013. <http://www.hobbyfarms.com/>.

Kinder Goat Breeders Association. Web. 10 Sept. 2013 <http://kindergoatbreeders.com/>.

Kinsey's Agricultural Services, Soil Fertility Consultants, Web. 10 Sept. 2013. <http://kinseyag.com/>.

Lehman's, (retail source for non-electric products), P.O. Box 270, Kidron, OH, 888-438-5346, Web. 10 Sept. 2013, <http://www.lehmans.com/>.

Maximizer Corn Sheller, Pleasant Hill Grain. Web. 17 Oct. 2013 <http://www.pleasanthillgrain.com/corn_sheller_hand_operated_crank_manual_antique_walnut_stationary.aspx>

Metal Roofing Source (for DIY metal roofing). Web. 10 Sept. 2013 <http://www.metalroofingsource.com/>

Pea Sheller, Jr. (Mr. Pea Sheller) Lee Manufacturing Company. Web. 17 Oct. 2013 <http://leemfgco.com/Item/Pea-Sheller-Jr>

Ray Peat, Web. 10 Sept. 2013. <http://raypeat.com/articles/>.

Tattler Reusable Canning Lids, Web, 10 Sept. 2013, <http://www.reusablecanninglids.com/>.

U.S. Department of Energy, "Wind Powering America". (wind resource map) Web. 09 Mar. 2013. <http://www.windpoweringamerica.gov/wind_maps.asp>.

YouTube, video sharing website. Web. 10 Sept. 2013. <www.youtube.com>

Wikipedia The Free Encyclopedia, "Hobby Farm" 21 Nov 2009. Web. 10 Sept. 2013. <http://en.wikipedia.org/wiki/Hobby_farm>.

Woodstock Soapstone Company, (Woodburning heat stove). Web. 10 Sept 2013. <http://www.woodstove.com/>.

Calculating Protein with the Pearson Square

The Pearson Square is a tool that can be used to calculate the amounts of any two components needed for a particular mix. It was originally developed to standardize the amounts of fat and protein in commercially produced milk. Since then, it has been used for wine making, juice mixing, cheese making, baking, and of course, feed formulation. It can be used for any animal and any nutrient, most commonly, protein.

There are numerous online calculators one can use, which are probably less intimidating for the mathematically challenged. However, the math is honestly quite simple. For two components it only requires subtraction. What you will need to know is the percentage of protein you're aiming for and the protein content of the grains or feedstuffs you have. This information will be listed as minimum crude protein on the feed bag label. Alternatively, many books and websites have charts which list these. I use the "Average Composition of Goat Feeds" chart[1] in Jerry Belanger's *Raising Milk Goats The Modern Way*. The various charts are not necessarily consistent, so for accuracy, any feed can be tested for its protein content by your state cooperative extension service.

PROBLEM: I need a feed mix containing 16% crude protein (CP). I have whole wheat berries and cowpeas. How much of each do I need?

STEP 1: Write the target amount (16%) in the middle of the square.

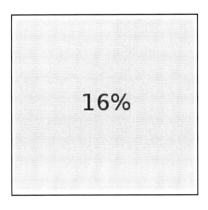

STEP 2: Values for the feedstuffs are placed at left hand corners.

RULE: *The number in the middle of the square must be between the numbers at the corners.*

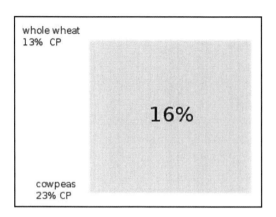

whole wheat
13% CP

16%

cowpeas
23% CP

According to the rule, my target crude protein must be between the crude protein levels of the items I'm mixing. Here, 16% is numerically between 13% and 23%, so I'm good to go.

STEP 3: Find the differences across the diagonal by subtracting the lower number from the higher.

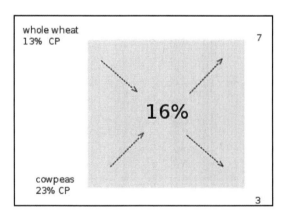

whole wheat
13% CP   7

16%

cowpeas
23% CP
                                          3

Number order doesn't matter, just the difference. In the example above, 16 – 13 = 3 and 23 – 16 = 7. Write these in the right hand corners across the diagonal.

STEP 4: Look across the horizontal legs of the square for the parts needed for the ration.

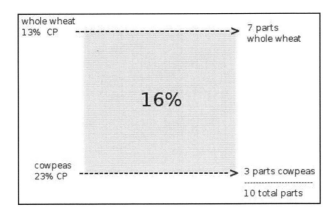

Looking from left to right, I would need 7 parts whole wheat and 3 parts cowpeas to get a 16% crude protein ration. The parts here can be thought of as weights.

SOLUTION. For 100 pounds of feed mix containing 16% crude protein, I would mix 70 pounds (7 parts) of whole wheat and 30 pounds (3 parts) of cowpeas.

So far so good? Obviously the Pearson Square is very useful if only two ingredients are involved. But what if I have more? What if one year I harvest 100 pounds of wheat (13% CP), 50 pounds of grain sorghum (10% CP), 90 pounds of cowpeas (23% CP), and 45 pounds of black oil sunflower seeds (16% CP). How would I know what amounts to mix to get my 16%?

A problem like this is a little trickier. I would need to make two mixes first, calculate the crude protein in each mix, and then use the Pearson Square to calculate how much I'd need of each mix. The wheat and grain sorghum could be combined as mix #1, my grain mix, while the cowpeas and black oil sunflower seeds (BOSS) would be mix #2, my protein supplement.

The math is a little more complicated here, because we first have to calculate percentages, which requires multiplication and division. Taken step by step, it not impossible. There is a formula to do it by hand, or one can use any calculator, including numerous online percentage calculators.

PROBLEM: Determine the amounts needed to make a 16% crude protein feed mix with the four ingredients mentioned previously.

STEP 1: Divide the ingredients into two groups. In this example, I'm going combine the wheat and grain sorghum and call them my grain mix. The cowpeas and BOSS (black oil sunflower seeds) will become my supplement mixture.

STEP 2: Find the total weight for each group. I'll start with my grain mix.

---

100 lb wheat + 50 lb sorghum = 150 lb

STEP 3: Find the percentage of each ingredient in the mix.

> **NOTE:** *A percent is a part of a whole. It can be written in one of two ways: with a percent sign (%) or as a decimal. Think of dollars and cents. 50 cents is half, or 50%, of a dollar. It is commonly written in its decimal form as $0.50 or .50. 25 cents would be 25% of a dollar or .25, 70 cents would be 70% of a dollar or .70.*

100 lbs of wheat is what % of 150 lbs? The formula looks like this

$$\frac{part}{whole} = \frac{\% \ of}{100}$$

> *Divide the part by the whole to find percentage. Here, divide the weight of the wheat by the weight of the whole mix. 100 divided by 150 = .666. This is its decimal form. For it's percent form, round up to 67%. 100 lbs of wheat is 67% of my 150 lb mix*
>
> *50 lbs of grain sorghum is what % of my 150 lb grain mix? 50 divided by 150 is .333. Rounded down, it's 33%. 50 lb of grain sorghum would be 33% of my mix.*

CHECK: 67% wheat + 33% sorghum = 100% grain mix

STEP 4: Repeat the same procedure for the supplement mixture.

STEP 5: Find the percent of protein for the grain mixture. The formula is:

> % of ingredient x its % protein
> + % of ingredient x its % protein
> ──────────────────────────────
> % crude protein in grain mix

I showed you how to calculate the percentages of wheat and grain sorghum in step 3. I plug these into the above formula.

> 67% (.67) wheat x 13% (.13) CP = (.087) 9%
> + 33% (.33) sorghum x 10% (.10) CP = (.033) 3%
> ──────────────────────────────
> crude protein in grain mix of 0.12 or 12%

Don't let the .087 confuse you. Think dollars and cents: 8 cents would be .08, and 9 cents would be .09. The .087 lies somewhere in between and is easily rounded up to 0.9 or 9%.

This tells me that my grain mixture of wheat and grain sorghum is 12% crude protein. I'll follow the same steps for my supplement mixture of cowpeas and BOSS. Try that one yourself. The answer is 20% crude protein.

STEP 6: Plug these numbers into the Pearson Square.

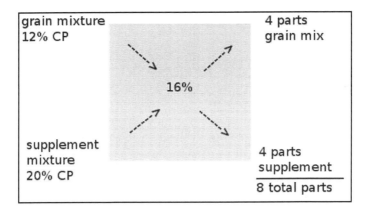

SOLUTION: The equal number of parts in my final mix means I have a 50/50 mix of the grain mixture and the supplement mixture. I would mix 50 pounds of each to get 100 pounds feed mix.

Although I used protein in these examples, anything could be calculated, calcium in a feed ration, for example. The possibilities are endless.

NOTES

[1]Jerry Belanger, *Raising Milk Goats The Modern Way* (Pownal, VT: Story Communications, Inc. 1994) 60-61

HOMEGROWN VITAMINS AND MINERALS FOR GOATS

This information was first published on my blog, and is reprinted here as a relevant resource. It has been updated, amended, and is, I hope, useful.

One of my self-sufficiency goals is to feed our animals from our land. This includes not only hay, forage, and grains, but also vitamins and minerals. Ideally, animals should get these from a natural forage diet. Most soils, unfortunately, have become depleted over the years, so that foraging alone rarely meets their needs. Nowadays, the common practice is to feed commercial feeds; pellets complete with protein, fats, carbohydrates, vitamins and minerals. Many goat owners also purchase vitamin and mineral supplements, and deficiencies are an ongoing topic on many goat discussion lists and forums. I've dealt with them too, and because of our poor soil, have gradually added items to my goats' diet to include a loose goat mineral, yeast culture, and Thorvin Kelp.

The question for me is, how can I provide the necessary vitamins and minerals myself? Besides our self-sufficiency goal, the cost does add up, especially for things I can't get locally such as kelp. Shipping is expensive, but also, several times I've had to wait when items were on back order.

Remineralizing our soil is one thing we are doing (see Chapter 7, "Food Self-Sufficiency: Feeding Our Animals"). Also, I have been researching how to grow my own vitamin and mineral supplements; vegetables and herbs that I can feed either fresh or dry as a top dressing on their food. This is what you'll find listed below. I won't say it's a complete list, but it's a start. Neither is it universal, I am mostly listing things I can grow or find in my area. And of course, the usual disclaimers apply.

VITAMINS

VITAMIN A & BetaCarotene. Basil, beet greens, butternut squash, cantaloupe, carrots, chickweed, collard greens, dandelion, dill, grape leaves, kale, marjoram, mustard, oregano, thyme (fresh), parsley, spinach, and sweet potatoes.

B VITAMINS. Goats are able to synthesize their own B vitamins, but deficiencies can occur and need to be addressed. A B12 deficiency can be a problem if the diet is not adequate in cobalt. Thiamin shortages are associated with polioencephalomalacia (goat polio). Off-flavored milk can often be corrected by adding B vitamins to the diet. The following foods are rich in B vitamins and may help avoid these problems.

B1 (THIAMIN). Kudzu, rosemary, seeds (sesame, sunflower), dried sage*, thyme, and yeast extract.

B2 (RIBOFLAVIN). Kudzu, parsley, sesame seeds, spearmint, wheat bran, yeast extract.

B3 (NIACIN). Bran (rice and wheat), kudzu, and yeast extract.

B5 (PANTOTHENIC ACID). Bran (rice and wheat), sunflower seeds

B6 (PYRIDOXINE). Bananas, bran (rice and wheat), dried herbs (basil, chives, dill, garlic, marjoram, oregano, rosemary, sage*, savory, spearmint, and tarragon), molasses, and seeds (sesame, sunflower).

B9 (FOLATE). Bananas, broccoli, cantaloupe, cowpeas, dried herbs (basil, chervil, marjoram, parsley, rosemary, spearmint, and thyme), endive, flax seeds, greens (collard, spinach, turnips), sunflower seeds, wheat germ, and yeast extract.

B12 (COBALAMIN). There are no plant sources for vitamin B12. However, goats can synthesize their own B12 if cobalt is in their diet. Plant sources include green leafy vegetables and comfrey.

VITAMIN C. This one can also be synthesized by livestock, although extra vitamin C is often given to help relieve udder congestion. Sources include: basil, beet greens, borage, broccoli, cabbage, cantaloupe (fruit, seeds, and rinds), citrus rinds, cleavers, kale, mint, mustard, rose hips, rosemary, thyme, parsley, and tomatoes (fruis only).

VITAMIN D. Sunshine

VITAMIN E. Basil, oregano, parsley, sage*, sunflower seeds, and thyme.

VITAMIN K is another vitamin goats can synthesize for themselves. Sources include basil, beet, blackberries, blueberries, broccoli, cabbage, carrots, collards, cucumber, dandelion, figs, kale, marjoram, mustard, oregano, parsley, raspberries, sage*, Swiss Chard, thyme, and turnip greens.

MINERALS

Some minerals can be toxic in excessive amounts: copper, selenium, and sulfur for example. All of these are found in minute amounts in common foods. My hope is that by remineralizing our soil, and feeding a variety of these common herbs and plants, I can prevent mineral deficiencies and not have to rely on comercial preparations.

CALCIUM. Amaranth leaves, basil, borage, celery seed, chamomile, chervil, chicory, cleavers, collards, coltsfoot, comfrey, coriander seed, dandelion, dill, fennel, flax seeds, greens (beet, turnip), horsetail, kale, kudzu, marjoram, mustard, oregano, parsley, plantain, poppy seed, rosemary, sage*, savory, sesame seeds, sorrel, spearmint, thyme, and willow.

COBALT is the precursor to vitamin B12, and goats can synthesize their own B12 if they get cobalt in their diet. I have not been able to find a specific list of goat acceptable foods that are rich in cobalt (i.e. vegan). Several places vaguely mention green leafy vegetables and pulses, but cobalt is usually found in animal foods, which goats do not eat. As with all minerals, plants can only take up what is available in the soil, which is why we're including cobalt in our remineralization program. My goats currently get their cobalt from their goat minerals.

COPPER. Basil (dried), burdock, chickweed, chicory, cleavers, coriander leaf, dandelion, dill, fennel, fennel seed, garlic, horseradish, marjoram, oregano, parsley, pumpkin and squash seeds, savory, sesame seeds, sorrel, spearmint, sunflower seeds, thyme, and yarrow.

IODINE. Seaweed. Commonly Thorvin Kelp is offered to goats, and iodine is apparently found in asparagus, cleavers, and garlic.

IRON. Asparagus, bamboo, basil, beet greens, blackberry, burdock, chervil, chicory, comfrey, coriander, dandelion, dill, kudzu, marjoram, nettle, oregano, parsley, raspberry, rose, rosemary, savory, skullcap, spearmint, strawberry, tarragon, thyme, turmeric, vervain, wormwood, and seeds: anise, cumin, fenugreek, pumpkin, sesame, squash, and sunflower.

MAGNESIUM. Basil, bran (oat, rice, wheat), carrot leaves, coriander, dandelion, dill, hops, marjoram, marshmallow, meadowsweet, molasses, mullein, oak, oregano, parsley, rose, sage*, savory, seeds (fennel, flax, pumpkin, squash, watermelon, sesame, and sunflower), slippery elm, spearmint, and thyme.

MANGANESE. Bamboo, basil, bran (oat, rice, wheat), coriander, dill, fennel, ginger (dried), marjoram, oregano, parsley, savory, seeds (pumpkin, squash, sesame, and sunflower), spearmint, thyme, and wheat germ.

MOLYBDENUM. Legumes, grains, and sunflower seeds.

PHOSPHOROUS. Bran, chickweed, dill, golden rod, marigold, seeds (flax, pumpkin, sesame, squash, and sunflower), and wheat germ. [Note: pregnant does need a particular calcium to phosphorous ratio of 2 parts calcium to 1 part phosphorous to prevent hypocalcemia or "milk fever".]

POTASSIUM. Bananas, basil, borage, carrot leaves, chamomile, chervil, collards, coriander leaves, couch grass, cucumber, dandelion, dill, elder, ginger, honeysuckle, kale, marjoram, meadowsweet, molasses, mullein, nettle, oak, oregano, parsley, peppermint, plantain, rice bran, seeds (squash, pumpkin, sunflower, watermelon, fennel), skullcap, spearmint, spinach, Swiss chard, and wormwood.

SELENIUM. Bran (oat, rice, wheat), chervil, coriander, dill seed, garlic, fenugreek, ginger, parsley, and sunflower seeds.

SODIUM. Cleavers, clover, comfrey, dill, fennel, garlic, marshmallow, nettle, violet, and woodruff.

SULFUR. Barley, cabbage, horseradish, kale, molasses, nuts, and seeds.

ZINC. Basil, buckwheat, chervil, coriander, dill and fennel seeds, ginger, parsley, pumpkin and squash seeds, sage*, savory, sesame seeds, thyme, watermelon seeds, and wheat germ.

*Sage is commonly used to decrease milk supply, so it should be avoided for does in milk.

There are no specific dosages for these because, as far as I know, none exist. All can be found on the lists of plants safe for goats to eat, and they will readily eat them as they browse. Mixed herbs as top dressings are usually sprinkled on top of grain rations in the amounts of teaspoons or tablespoons.

BIBLIOGRAPHY & ADDITIONAL RESOURCES

BOOKS

Adabie, M.J., *The Everything Herbal Remedies Book*. Holbrook, MA: Adams Media Corporation, 2000.

Colby, Pat, *Natural Goat Care*. Austin, TX: Acres U.S.A., 2001.

de Bairacli Levy, Juliette, *The Complete Herbal Handbook For Farm And Stable*. London: Faber and Faber Ltd., 1991.

Morrison, F. B., *Feeds And Feeding: A Handbook for the Student and Stockman*. Ithaca, NY: The Morrison Publishing Co., 1943

Ody, Penelopy, *The Complete Medicinal Herbal*. New York: Dorling Kindersley, 1993.

WEBSITES

Administrator-GL "Minerals and Mineral Deficiencies." *Goat-Link*. 23 April 2010 Web. 11 Sept. 2013. <goat-link.com/content/view/214/210/>

Lewis, Daphne. "Nutrition." *Bamboo Farming USA*. Web. 11 Sept. 2013. <http://www.bamboofarmingusa.com/Fodder.html>.

Livestrong.com. Web. 11 Sept. 2013 <http://www.livestrong.com/>.

Miller, Kristie. "Herbal Mineral Information." *Land of Havilah Farm*. Web. 11 Sept. 2013 <www.landofhavilahfarm.com/goat-minerals.htm>

Reith, Sue. "Hypocalcemia – Feed for Prevention." *Dairy Goat Care and Management*. 5 Jan. 2007. Web. 09 Mar. 2013. <goats.wetpaint.com/page/Hypocalcemia+-+Feed+for+Prevention>.

"Spice And Mineral Guide", *The Third Age*. Web. 11 Sept. 2013 <www.thirdage.com/nc/fgm/spice-and-herb-minerals-200>.

Waltz, Lisa. Dr. "Basic Healing Herbs For Goats." *Waltz's Ark*. Web. 09 Mar. 2013.<www.naturalark.com/natherbgoat.html>.

(Willd.) Sanjappa & Pradeep."Pueraria montana lobata", *Plants For A Future*. Web. 11 Sept. 2013. <http://www.pfaf.org/user/Plant.aspx? LatinName=Pueraria+montana+lobata>.

INDEX

Page numbers in *italics* indicate photographs, illustrations, or captions.

15362959R00148

Made in the USA
San Bernardino, CA
22 September 2014